THE LANDLORD'S LEGAL GUIDE IN PENNSYLVANIA

Rebecca A. DeSimone
Attorney at Law

SPHINX® PUBLISHING
AN IMPRINT OF SOURCEBOOKS, INC.®
NAPERVILLE, ILLINOIS
www.SphinxLegal.com

First Edition, 2003

Published by: **Sphinx® Publishing, An Imprint of Sourcebooks, Inc.®**

<u>Naperville Office</u>
P.O. Box 4410
Naperville, Illinois 60567-4410
630-961-3900
Fax: 630-961-2168
www.sourcebooks.com
www.SphinxLegal.com

This publication is designed to provide accurate and authoritative information in regard to the subject matter covered. It is sold with the understanding that the publisher is not engaged in rendering legal, accounting, or other professional service. If legal advice or other expert assistance is required, the services of a competent professional person should be sought.

From a Declaration of Principles Jointly Adopted by a Committee of the
American Bar Association and a Committee of Publishers and Associations

This product is not a substitute for legal advice.

Disclaimer required by Texas statutes.

Library of Congress Cataloging-in-Publication Data
DeSimone, Rebecca A., 1963–
    The landlord's legal guide in Pennsylvania / by Rebecca A. DeSimone
-- 1st ed.
            p. cm.
Includes index.
    ISBN 1-57248-245-1 (pbk.)
  1. Landlord and tenant--Pennsylvania--Popular works. 2. Landlord and
tenant--Pennsylvania--Forms. I. DeSimone, Rebecca A. II. Title.

KFP117.Z9 D47 2002
346.74804'34--dc21
                                                    2002012369

Printed and bound in the United States of America.
VHG Paperback — 10 9 8 7 6 5 4 3 2 1

CONTENTS

USING SELF-HELP LAW BOOKS

Before using a self-help law book, you should realize the advantages and disadvantages of doing your own legal work and understand the challenges and diligence that this requires.

THE GROWING TREND

Rest assured that you won't be the first or only person handling your own legal matter. For example, in some states, more than seventy-five percent of divorces and other cases have at least one party representing him or herself. Because of the high cost of legal services, this is a major trend and many courts are struggling to make it easier for people to represent themselves. However, some courts are not happy with people who do not use attorneys and refuse to help them in any way. For some, the attitude is, "Go to the law library and figure it out for yourself."

We at Sphinx write and publish self-help law books to give people an alternative to the often complicated and confusing legal books found in most law libraries. We have made the explanations of the law as simple and easy to understand as possible. Of course, unlike an attorney advising an individual client, we cannot cover every conceivable possibility.

COST/VALUE ANALYSIS

Whenever you shop for a product or service, you are faced with various levels of quality and price. In deciding what product or service to buy, you make a cost/value analysis on the basis of your willingness to pay and the quality you desire.

When buying a car, you decide whether you want transportation, comfort, status, or sex appeal. Accordingly, you decide among such choices as a Neon, a Lincoln, a Rolls Royce, or a Porsche. Before making a decision, you usually weigh the merits of each option against the cost.

When you get a headache, you can take a pain reliever (such as aspirin) or visit a medical specialist for a neurological examination. Given this choice, most people, of course, take a pain reliever, since it costs only pennies; whereas a medical examination costs hundreds of dollars and takes a lot of time. This is usually a logical choice because it is rare to need anything more than a pain reliever for a headache. But in some cases, a headache may indicate a brain tumor and failing to see a specialist right away can result in complications. Should everyone with a headache go to a specialist? Of course not, but people treating their own illnesses must realize that they are betting on the basis of their cost/value analysis of the situation. They are taking the most logical option.

The same cost/value analysis must be made when deciding to do one's own legal work. Many legal situations are very straight forward, requiring a simple form and no complicated analysis. Anyone with a little intelligence and a book of instructions can handle the matter without outside help.

But there is always the chance that complications are involved that only an attorney would notice. To simplify the law into a book like this, several legal cases often must be condensed into a single sentence or paragraph. Otherwise, the book would be several hundred pages long and too complicated for most people. However, this simplification necessarily leaves out many details and nuances that would apply to special or unusual situations. Also, there are many ways to interpret most legal questions. Your case may come before a judge who disagrees with the analysis of our authors.

Therefore, in deciding to use a self-help law book and to do your own legal work, you must realize that you are making a cost/value analysis. You have decided that the money you will save in doing it yourself outweighs the chance that your case will not turn out to your satisfaction. Most people handling their own simple legal matters never have a problem, but occasionally people find that it ended up costing them more to have an attorney straighten out the situation than it would have if they had hired an attorney in the beginning. Keep this in mind if you decide to handle your own case, and be sure to consult an attorney if you feel you might need further guidance.

LOCAL RULES   The next thing to remember is that a book that covers the law for the entire nation, or even for an entire state, cannot possibly include every procedural difference of every county court. Whenever possible, we provide the exact form needed; however, in some areas, each county, or even each judge, may require unique forms and procedures. In our *state* books, our forms usually cover the majority of counties in the state, or provide examples of the type of form that will be required. In our *national* books, our forms are sometimes even more general in nature but are designed to give a good idea of the type of form that will be needed in most locations. Nonetheless, keep in mind that your *state*, county, or judge may have a requirement, or use a form, that is not included in this book.

You should not necessarily expect to be able to get all of the information and resources you need solely from within the pages of this book. This book will serve as your guide, giving you specific information whenever possible and helping you to find out what else you will need to know. This is just like if you decided to build your own backyard deck. You might purchase a book on how to build decks. However, such a book would not include the building codes and permit requirements of every city, town, county, and township in the nation; nor would it include the lumber, nails, saws, hammers, and other materials and tools you would need to actually build the deck. You would use the book as your guide, and then do some work and research involving such matters as whether you need a permit of some kind, what type and grade of wood are available in your area, whether to use hand tools or power tools, and how to use those tools.

Before using the forms in a book like this, you should check with your court clerk to see if there are any local rules of which you should be aware, or local forms you will need to use. Often, such forms will require the same information as the forms in the book but are merely laid out differently, use slightly different language, or use different color paper so the clerks can easily find them. They will sometimes require additional information.

CHANGES IN THE LAW

Besides being subject to state and local rules and practices, the law is subject to change at any time. The courts and the legislatures of all fifty states are constantly revising the laws. It is possible that while you are reading this book, some aspect of the law is being changed or a court is interpreting a law in a different way. You should always check the most recent statutes, rules and regulations to see what, if any changes have been made.

In most cases, the change will be of minimal significance. A form will be redesigned, additional information will be required, or a waiting period will be extended. As a result, you might need to revise a form, file an extra form, or wait out a longer time period; these types of changes will not usually affect the outcome of your case. On the other hand, sometimes a major part of the law is changed, the entire law in a particular area is rewritten, or a case that was the basis of a central legal point is overruled. In such instances, your entire ability to pursue your case may be impaired.

Again, you should weigh the value of your case against the cost of an attorney and make a decision as to what you believe is in your best interest.

INTRODUCTION

Proceeding through a landlord/tenant case is, in all probability, a common and disturbing encounter within the legal system. At a time, as a business owner or small landholder, when you are least likely to possess extra funds, paying a lawyer to handle a landlord/tenant matter can be an unwanted bill to pay. In a landlord/tenant case, it is not uncommon for the parties to incur legal bills of over $5,000. Horror stories abound of landlord/tenant matters causing delay and headaches for property owners and it is not uncommon for lawyers to charge substantial fees to handle such cases.

This book is intended to give you an overview of landlord/tenant law and enable you to proceed through the landlord/tenant maze without the need to hire an attorney. It is a guide that endeavors to eliminate complicated and verbose legal and technical words, creating an easier, user-friendly instruction booklet. Even if you do choose to hire a lawyer, this book will assist and guide you in more effectively working with him or her, which can reduce your overall legal fee. Furthermore, this book will provide you with a first-rate outline and sound advice that will aid you in the understanding of all aspects of landlord/tenant situations and lease agreement drafting in the Commonwealth of Pennsylvania.

Because the law is constantly changing, it is a good idea to check with a lawyer it you have a specific question. In addition, if you should have specific problems or want further information, contact an attorney. Legal services are available for persons who cannot afford an attorney and can be found in your yellow pages.

To be sure, this is not a law school course. It is rather, a practical guide to move you through the landlord/tenant "system" as easily as possible. Most of the legal terminology has been eliminated. However, some legal words are defined in the Glossary at the end of the book. For ease of understanding, this book uses the term "lessor" or "landlord" to refer to the land or property owner and the term "lessee" or "tenant" to refer to the land or property occupier or renter. Gender selections have been made for ease of discussion and in no way are meant to suggest preference or standard.

In most counties, landlord/tenant cases are filed with the District Justice office. Please bear in mind that different district justices and courts in different counties, may have their own particular procedures, forms, and ways of handling matters. The district justice court in your particular township can inform you if they have any special forms or requirements. Personnel at the district justice office cannot give legal advice (they are not permitted to do so) however they can apprise you of what their court or district justice requires.

The first chapter of this book provides you with a comprehensive overview of the relevant landlord/tenant laws and the legal system. Chapter 2 aids you in your evaluation of whether you wish to hire an attorney. Chapters 3 discusses the landlord/tenant relationship. Chapter 4 explains the way in which residential lease agreements are created and elaborates upon various aspects of proper drafting and protective clauses. Chapter 5 discusses Standard Form Leases from the landlord's perspective. Chapter 6 addresses the primary considerations of federally supported, financially Subsidized Low Income Housing Programs.

Each of these chapters will aid you in evaluating your situation and provide you with an idea of what you should expect should you decide to proceed with a landlord/tenant matter. The remaining portion of this book contains the forms you will need to undertake a landlord/tenant action or to draft lease agreements. Appendix A contains selected portions of the Pennsylvania law dealing with landlord/tenant issues. Although these provisions are discussed in the book, it is sometimes helpful to read the law exactly as it is written. Appendix B contains checklists of the documents you may need to prepare and file in various types of landlord/tenant procedures.

You will not need to use all of the forms. This book will tell you which forms you need, depending upon your situation, and will guide you in filling in the necessary information. A helpful Glossary is also provided for your better understanding of processes and procedures.

Fundamentals of Landlord/Tenant Law

1

The landlord/tenant affiliation is founded upon duties described in either statutory law, the common law (law derived from our founding days as developed and brought to this country from England), or the individual lease. Provisions which may be contained in a lease are normally regulated by statutory law. (See Section 1.403 of the (URLTA).)

Basic to all leases is the implied "covenant of quiet enjoyment." This covenant ensures the tenant that his possession will not be disturbed by someone with a superior legal title to the land including the landlord. A breach of the "covenant of quiet enjoyment" may result in actual or constructive eviction.

A constructive eviction occurs when the landlord causes the premises to become uninhabitable. An actual eviction occurs when some action of the tenant causes a legal eviction proceeding to occur.

We commonly use the words "landlord and tenant" to describe modern interests in real estate (property or land). However, estates in land are traditionally divided into "freehold" and "non-freehold," also termed "leasehold." For the purposes of this book, a property owner is generally believed to have a "freehold" interest, while a tenant has a "leasehold" interest in the land. Leasehold estates have one particularly important characteristic. They each normally include a *duty on the tenant's part to pay rent*. Since modern statutes did not specifically define who is a tenant, courts had to determine the legislature's meaning. (*Nelson v. Grays* 531 N.W. 2d~26 1995. Also see: *Grant v. Detroit Association of Woman's Clubs.* 505 N.W. 2d. 254 1993.*)

One other important characteristic of a leasehold is that the tenant, for the term of the lease, is entitled to *exclusive possession*. This distinguishes a leasehold from several other types of property interests. For instance, a guest in a hotel does not normally have a leasehold interest, but rather, a *license to use the property*. The same is true of a lodger in a boarding house. Consequently, statutes applicable to landlord/tenant relations may not apply and the hotel keeper may have the right to use *self-help* to evict a non-paying guest even though such self-help is now forbidden by statute to landlords.

Housing codes were established to regulate occupancy standards and ensure that residential rental units were habitable at the time of rental and during the tenancy. Depending on the state, housing code violations may lead to administrative action or to the tenant being allowed to withhold rent.

HOUSING CODES
The habitability of a residential rental unit is also ensured by *warranties of habitability* which are prescribed by common and/or statutory law. (see Section 2.104 of the (URLTA).) A breach of the warranty of habitability or a covenant within the lease may constitute constructive eviction, allow the tenant to withhold rent, repair the problem and deduct the cost from the rent, or recover damages. (see (URLTA) Sections 4.101, 4.104, and 4.105.)

Unless the lease states otherwise, there is an assumption that the *tenant has a duty* to pay rent. State statutes may provide for a reasonable rental value to be paid absent a rental price provision. (see (ULTRA) Section 1.401(b).) In commercial leases, rent is commonly calculated in part or whole as a percentage of the tenant's sales.

RENT
Rent acceleration clauses that cause all the rent to become due if the tenant breaches a provision of the lease are common in both residential and commercial leases.

EVICTION

Summary eviction statutes commonly allow a landlord to quickly evict a tenant who breaches statutorily specified lease provisions, particularly a failure to pay rent. *Self-help*, a unilateral landlord action, as a method of eviction is now usually prohibited. Some states do not even allow it for tenants who have held over after the end of a lease. (see (URLTA) Sec. 4.207, and Restatement 2d. Sec. 14.2.) Landlords are also restricted from evicting tenants in retaliation of action the tenant took to enforce a provision of the lease or applicable law. (See (URLTA) Sec. 4.197, and 5.101.)

REFUND OF DEPOSITS

Case law in Pennsylvania sets out quite specific requirements for refunding of deposits, including whether they should be held in interest-bearing accounts. You can check Pa. Stat. Ann. tit. 68, Sections 250.511 a–.512, which provides all of the pertinent information that you will need regarding issues that involve retaining the security deposit of the tenant.

LANDLORD'S RESPONSIBILITY

In Pennsylvania, a landlord's general responsibility can be summarized as a duty to:

- put and keep the premises in a fit and habitable condition;

- maintain the common areas of buildings and grounds in safe and sanitary condition;

- comply with building, housing, health, and safety codes;

- keep all electrical, plumbing, heating, and ventilation systems and fixtures in good working order;

- maintain all appliances and equipment supplied or required to be supplied by the landlord;

- provide running water and reasonable amounts of hot water and heat, unless the hot water and heat are supplied by an installation that is under the exclusive control of the tenant and supplied by a direct public utility hook-up;

- provide garbage cans and arrange for trash removal if the landlord owns four or more residential units in the same building. (Some jurisdictions also require recycling containers);

- give at least 24-hours notice, unless it is an emergency, before entering a tenant's unit, and enter only at reasonable times and in a reasonable manner; and,

- evict the tenant when informed by a law enforcement officer of drug activity by the tenant, a member of the tenant's household, or a guest of the tenant occurring in or otherwise connected with the tenant's premises.

TENANT'S
RESPONSIBILITY

In Pennsylvania, a tenant's general responsibility can be summarized as a duty to:

- keep the premises safe and sanitary;

- dispose of rubbish in the proper manner;

- keep the plumbing fixtures as clean as their condition permits;

- use electrical and plumbing fixtures properly;

- comply with housing, health, and safety codes that apply to tenants;

- refrain from damaging the premises and keep guests from causing damage;

- maintain appliances supplied by the landlord in good working order;

- conduct self in a manner that does not disturb any neighbors and require guests to do the same;

- permit landlord to enter the dwelling unit if the request is reasonable and proper notice is given; and,

- comply with state or municipal drug laws in connection with the premises and require household members and guests to do likewise.

LAWYERS 2

Whether you need an attorney will depend upon many factors, such as how comfortable you feel handling the matter yourself, whether your situation is more complicated than usual, and how much opposition you get from your opponent. It may be advisable to hire an attorney if you encounter a judge with a hostile attitude, or if your opponent gets a lawyer who wants to fight. There are no court appointed lawyers in landlord/tenant cases, so if you want an attorney, you will have to hire one.

A general rule is that you should consider hiring an attorney whenever you reach a point where you no longer feel comfortable representing yourself. This point will vary greatly with each person, so there is no easy way to be more definite.

A more appropriate question is: "Do you want a lawyer?" The next section will discuss some of the "pros" and "cons" of hiring a lawyer, and some of the elements you may wish to consider in making this decision.

LAWYER FEES

One of the first questions you will want to consider, and most likely the reason you are reading this book, is: "How much will an attorney cost?"

Attorneys come in all ages, shapes, sizes, sexes, racial and ethnic groups—and also price ranges. As a rough estimate, you can expect an attorney to charge anywhere from $250 to $2,000 for a less complicated landlord/tenant issues, and $800 and up for a more complicated problem. Lawyers usually charge an hourly rate ranging from about $75 to $300 per hour.

ADVANTAGES TO
HIRING A LAWYER

The following are some advantages to hiring a lawyer.

Judges and other attorneys may take you more seriously. Most judges prefer both parties to have attorneys. They feel this helps the case move in a more orderly fashion because both sides will know the procedures and relevant issues. Persons representing themselves very often waste a lot of time on matters that have little bearing on the outcome of the case.

A lawyer will serve as a "buffer" between you and your opponent. This can lead to a quicker passage through the system by reducing the chance for emotions to take control and confuse the issues. For the same reasons that are listed above, attorneys prefer to deal with other attorneys. However, if you become familiar with this book, and conduct yourself in a calm and proper manner, you should have no trouble.

You can let your lawyer worry about all of the details. By having an attorney, you need only become generally familiar with the contents of this book, as it will be your attorney's job to file the proper papers in the correct form, and to deal with the *prothonotary* (court clerk), the judge, the process server, your opponent, and your opponent's attorney.

Lawyers provide professional assistance with problems. In the event your case is complicated, or suddenly becomes complicated, it is an advantage to have an attorney who is familiar with your case. It can also be comforting to have a lawyer to turn to for advice and for answers to your questions.

ADVANTAGES TO
REPRESENTING
YOURSELF

On the other hand, there are also advantages to representing yourself.

You save the cost of a lawyer. This is the most obvious advantage to representing yourself. If your case is a simple one, it probably is your best option to go it alone.

Sometimes judges feel more sympathetic toward a person not represented by an attorney. This sometimes results in the unrepresented person being allowed a certain amount of leeway with the procedure rules.

The procedure may be faster. Two of the most frequent complaints the bar association receives about lawyers involve delay in completing the case and failure to return phone calls. Most lawyers have a heavy caseload, which sometimes results in lapses of time in addressing cases. If you are following the progress of your own case you will be able to push it along the system diligently.

NOTE: *Selecting an attorney is not easy. However, as the next section discusses, it is important to know that you select an attorney with whom you will be happy.*

MIDDLE GROUND
You may want to look for an attorney who will be willing to accept an hourly fee to answer your questions and give you help as you need it. This way you will save some legal costs, but still receive some professional assistance. You will also establish a relationship with an attorney who will be somewhat familiar with your case in the event things become complicated and you need a full-time lawyer.

SELECTING A LAWYER

Selecting a lawyer is a two-step process. First, you need to decide with which attorney you will make an appointment. Secondly, you need to decide if you wish to hire *(retain)* that attorney.

ASK A FRIEND
A common, and frequently the best, way to find a lawyer is to ask someone you know to recommend one to you. This is especially helpful if the lawyer represented your friend in a landlord/tenant matter.

LAWYER REFERRAL SERVICE
You can find a referral service by looking in the yellow pages phone directory under "Attorney Referral Services" or "Attorneys." This is a service, usually operated by a bar association, that is designed to match a client with an attorney handling cases in the area of law the client needs. The referral service does not guarantee the quality of work, nor the level of experience or ability of the attorney. Finding a lawyer in this manner will at least connect you with one who is interested in landlord/tenant matters, and probably has some experience in this area.

YELLOW PAGES

Check under the heading for "Attorneys" in the yellow pages phone directory. Many of the lawyers and law firms will place display ads indicating their areas of practice, and educational backgrounds. Look for firms or lawyers that indicate they practice in areas such as "landlord/tenant." Big ads are not necessarily indicative of expertise.

ASK ANOTHER
LAWYER

If you have used the services of an attorney in the past for some other matter (for example, a real estate closing, traffic ticket, or a will), you may want to call and ask if he or she could refer you to an attorney whose ability in the area of landlord/tenant is respected.

EVALUATING A LAWYER

From your search, you should select three to five lawyers worthy of further consideration. Your first step will be to call each attorney's office, explain that you are interested in seeking representation and aid in a landlord/tenant matter, and ask the following questions:

- Does the attorney (or law firm) handle this type of matter?

- What is the fee range and what is the cost of an initial consultation? (Do not expect to get a definite answer on a landlord/tenant fee, but the attorney may be able to give you a range or an hourly rate. You will probably need to meet with the lawyer for anything more detailed.)

- How soon can you get an appointment? (Most offices require you to make an appointment.)

    During your first appointment, ask the attorney the following questions:

    - How much will it cost?
    - How will the fee be paid?
    - How long has the attorney been in practice?
    - How long has the attorney been in practice in Pennsylvania?

- What percentage of the attorney's cases involve landlord/tenant cases or matters? (Do not expect an exact answer, but you should get a rough estimate that reflects at least twenty percent.)
- How long will it take? (Do not expect an exact answer, but the attorney should be able to give you an average range and discuss things that may make a difference.)

If you get acceptable answers to these questions, it's time to ask yourself the following questions about the lawyer:

- Do you feel comfortable talking to the lawyer?

- Is the lawyer friendly toward you?

- Does the lawyer seem confident in himself or herself?

- Does the lawyer seem to be straight-forward with you, and able to explain issues so you understand?

If you get satisfactory answers to all of these questions, you probably have a lawyer with whom you will be happy to work. Most clients are happiest with an attorney with whom they feel comfortable.

WORKING WITH A LAWYER

In general, you will work best with your attorney if you keep an open, honest, and friendly attitude. Also, consider the following suggestions.

ASK QUESTIONS

If you want to know something or if you do not understand something, ask your attorney. If you do not understand the answer, tell your attorney and ask him or her to explain it again. You should not be embarrassed to ask questions. Many people who say they had a bad experience with a lawyer either did not ask enough questions or had a lawyer who would not take the time to explain things to them. If your lawyer is not taking the time to explain what he or she is doing, it may be time to look for a new lawyer.

GIVE COMPLETE
INFORMATION

Anything you tell your attorney is confidential. An attorney can lose his or her license to practice if he or she reveals information without your permission. So do not hold back. Tell your lawyer everything, even if it does not seem important to you. There are many things that seem unimportant to a non-attorney, but can change the outcome of a case. Also, do not hold something back because you are afraid it will hurt your case. It will definitely hurt your case if your lawyer does not find out about it until he or she hears it in court from your opponent's attorney. But if your lawyer knows in advance, he or she can plan to eliminate or reduce damage to your case.

ACCEPT
REALITY

Listen to what your lawyer tells you about the law and the system. It will do you no good to argue because the law or the system does not work the way you think it should. For example, if your lawyer tells you that the judge can not hear your case for two weeks, do not try demanding that he or she set a hearing tomorrow. By refusing to accept reality, you are only setting yourself up for disappointment. And remember: It is not your attorney's fault that the system is not perfect, or that the law does not say what you would like it to say.

BE PATIENT

The advice to be patient applies both to being patient with the system (which is often slow as we discussed earlier), as well as being patient with your attorney. Do not expect your lawyer to return your phone call within an hour. Your lawyer may not be able to return it the same day. Most lawyers are very busy. It is rare that an attorney can maintain a full caseload and still make each client feel as if he or she is the only client. Despite the popular trend toward "lawyer-bashing," remember that many lawyers are good people who wish to aid and assist the public.

TALK TO THE
SECRETARY

Your lawyer's secretary can be a valuable source of information. Be friendly and get to know the secretary. Often he or she will be able to answer your questions, and you will not get a bill for the time you talk to the secretary.

LET YOUR
ATTORNEY
HANDLE YOUR
OPPONENT

It is your lawyer's job to communicate with your opponent, or with your opponent's lawyer. Let your lawyer do his or her job. Many lawyers have had clients lose or damage their cases when the client decides to say or do something on his or her own.

BE ON TIME — The advice to be on time applies to both appointments with your lawyer and to court hearings.

KEEPING YOUR CASE MOVING — Many lawyers operate on the old principle of the "squeaking wheel gets the oil." Work on a case tends to be put off until a deadline is near, an emergency develops, or the client calls. There is a reason for this. Many lawyers take more cases than can be effectively handled in order to earn the income they desire. Your task is to become a squeaking wheel that does not squeak too much. Whenever you talk to your lawyer ask the following questions:

- What is the next step?

- When do you expect it to be done?

- When should I talk to you next?

Call your lawyer if you do not hear anything when you expect. Do not remind your lawyer of the missed call; just ask how things are going.

FIRING YOUR LAWYER

If you can no longer work with your lawyer, it is time to either go it alone or get a new attorney. You will need to send your lawyer a letter stating that you no longer desire his or her services and are discharging him or her from your case. Also state that you will be coming by his or her office the following day to pick up your file.

The attorney does not have to give you his or her own notes or other work he or she has in progress, but he or she must give you the essential contents of your file (such as copies of papers already filed or prepared and billed for, and any documents that you provided). If the lawyer refuses to give you your file, for any reason, contact the Pennsylvania Bar about filing a complaint, or grievance, against the lawyer. Of course, you will need to settle any remaining fees charged for work that has already been done by the lawyer.

OVERVIEW OF LEASE AGREEMENTS 3

The landlord/tenant relationship can be created in many ways. One of the most common methods, and one which is the most highly recommended is establishing the landlord/tenant relationship through the execution and use of a lease agreement.

WHAT IS A LEASE AGREEMENT

Pennsylvania Common Law identifies a *lease* as an agreement that creates the relationship between landlord and tenant. A lease is a contract giving possession of land or real estate to the tenant for a term in exchange for a rental fee. (*In re Wilson's Estate*, 349 Pa. 646, 37 A.2d 709, 710 (1944); *Morrisville Shopping Center v. Sun Ray Drug Co.*, 381 Pa. 576, 112 A.2d 183, 186 (1955).)

Pennsylvania *contract law* applies. Contract law focuses on the establishment of a landlord and tenant relationship. (*In re Wilson: SO Estate.*) Contract law also determines many of the continuing rights and liabilities under an established lease agreement. (*Pugh v. Holmes*, 486 Pa. 272, 284, 405 A.2d 897, 903 (1979).)

In entering into a lease, the tenant becomes the purchaser of a dwelling or land. The law of property regards the lease as equivalent to a sale of the premises for a term. (*Commonwealth v. Monumental Properties Inc.*, 459 Pa. 450, 329 A.2d 812, 822-823 (1974).)

EXPRESSLY ESTABLISHED OR IMPLIED LEASE AGREEMENTS

A lease can be one which is written (*expressly*) or one that is made by *oral* agreement. Existence of the landlord and tenant bond can also be implied from the *behavior* of the involved parties. (*Pagano v. Redevelopment Authority of City of Philadelphia*, 249 Pa. Super. 303, 376 A.2d 999 (1917).) This means that the landlord and tenant involved in the making of a lease agreement need not use any specific words to construct the landlord and tenant relationship. The word "lease" need not even be used. (*Bussman v. Ganster*, 72 Pa. 285 (1872); *Moore v. Miller*, 8 Pa. 272 (1848).)

📕 For example, in a particular situation, where the specifics demonstrated the goal of creating the lease and the involved parties paid and accepted a rental fee on a periodic basis, a *tenancy* was created on the basis of these actions. The landlord or tenant cannot later say there was no lease agreement without being held responsible for *damages* (money losses for breaking the contract). (*Nackles v. Union Real Estate Co. of Pittsburgh*, 415 Pa. 407, 204 A.2d 50, 51 (1964).)

📕 Whether a lease agreement has been created in a certain manner becomes a question of law for a court to determine. We suggest that you use an attorney if you find yourself in this situation. (*Lasher v. Redevelopment Authority of Allegheny County*, 211 Pa. Super. 408, 236 A.2d 831 (1967).)

PERIOD OF A LEASE AGREEMENT

A lease that is created for a term of more than three years must be written and it must be signed by the parties to the lease. Otherwise, it will be void. One should take note that the failure to abide by this requirement, even where a lease is designed to exist in excess of three years, does not void or destroy the landlord and tenant relationship. On the contrary, the flaw causes that part of the agreement exceeding three years to be *voidable* (possibly voided). Courts will still review and assess the actions of the involved parties to decide whether a form of *periodic tenancy*, or *limited term tenancy*, may be implied from the actions and undertakings of the parties. (*Ferri v. Liberatoscioli*, 338 Pa. 454, 456,13 A.2d 45 (1940).)

IMPLIED
LENGTH
OF LEASE

A lease may be created to exist for a specific term, or as a *tenancy-at-will*. This means the lease can be terminated at *any* time by *either* party. Under the old common law set of guidelines, courts implied a tenancy-at-will where the lease contract failed to state the duration of the lease. However, using the modern interpretation (that has existed for the last hundred years or so), Pennsylvania courts have little tendency to create an implied tenancy-at-will from a lease agreement which failed to specify a lease term. The same is true for a lease containing a specific term that has been determined to be unenforceable. (*Aaron v. Woodcock*, 283 Pa. 33 (1925); *Dunn v. Rothennel*, 112 Pa. 272, 282 (1886); Clark v. Smith, 25 Pa. 137, 140 (1855).)

Where there is no term specifically stating a duration of the tenancy in a lease agreement, Pennsylvania courts will then imply *renewable terms* from the periods for which rental payments had been reserved and paid. For instance, where a yearly rent is reserved and paid, courts imply a *one year tenancy*, and *year-to-year* if the tenant remains in possession after one year. (*Ferri v. Liberatoscioli* and. *Aaron v. Woodcock*.)

A tenancy-at-will is found currently, only in the rare occurrences where the lease agreement does not require any rental payments at all. No lease period can be implied from periodic payments. (*Lasher v. Redevelopment Authority of Allegheny County*, 211 Pa. Super. 408, 236 A.2d 831 (1967).) Once a landlord and tenant relationship has been fashioned, the relationship can be ended only by following the appropriate measures the law sets out for termination of leases. (*Snyder v. Carfrey*, 54 Pa. 90, 93 (1867).)

PERIODIC
TENANCIES

The majority of residential leases produce some form of *periodic tenancy*. A *periodic tenancy*, commonly known as week-to-week, month-to-month or year-to-year, is a tenancy that continues from one period to the next automatically, unless either party terminates it at the end of a period, by notice, which is usually the length of the rental period.

A periodic tenancy continues indefinitely, until terminated by one of the parties with proper notice that expires when it reaches the end of its stated term.

ORAL LEASE AGREEMENTS

ORAL LEASES

Oral agreements for rental of residential premises are perfectly valid and enforceable contracts, except if they exceed three years (as discussed previously). Oral leases occur frequently in dealings between low and moderate income landlords and tenants and between buyers and sellers of residential properties when settlement has been unexpectedly delayed. Most often the payment of rent on a monthly basis establishes that these agreements are *month-to-month* periodic tenancies. The actual negotiated agreement of the parties may cover few terms other than the amount of rent, the dates for payment, and the responsibility for utilities. The provisions of Pennsylvania common law and statutes must fill in the gaps in the agreement when disputes arise during the tenancy over the many issues not covered by the oral agreement.

BENEFITS FROM THE TENANT'S VIEW

Realty agents and their attorneys often draft written form lease agreements that include many burdensome terms. In a number of them, the tenant is required to *waive* (give up) every imaginable common law, statutory, and constitutional right that would otherwise exist for the benefit of the tenant. The tenant often has little power over the type of form lease that must be executed in order to take possession and to rent a certain dwelling unit, so the written lease that the tenant signs often will be skewed significantly against that tenant. In contrast, the general laws defending the tenant will remain in full effect under an oral lease agreement.

DRAWBACKS FROM THE TENANT'S VIEW

Of all the terms in the typical lease agreement, the amount of the rental fee and the duration of the lease agreement are by and large the most important. The tenant under an oral tenancy faces uncertainty as to both terms. Where the tenant has a strong interest in a long-term tenancy at a fixed rate, a written lease will provide an enforceable guarantee as to those terms. Most landlords are also concerned about these terms, and so prefer the written agreements to avoid the dispute of facts an oral lease may incur.

WRITTEN LEASES: RESIDENTIAL HOUSE LEASE

A residential house lease agreement is utilized by the home owner who is leasing the house to one or more persons as a *personal* (not business) residence.

Renting residential real estate properties is often a wise investment. The Internal Revenue Code still offers certain worthwhile tax benefits to owners of real estate who manage and lease the property on their own. Often, the leased house will produce income while providing the home owner a tax deduction.

A written lease agreement for those contemplating house leasing is a *must*. Terms of an oral lease are often unenforceable here. The Commonwealth of Pennsylvania requires that any agreement regarding an interest in real estate be in writing in order to be enforceable.

In addition, real property leasing poses distinctive cautions to the property owner, such as legal actions by the tenant or guests of the tenant for personal injuries while in, on, or visiting the property. Claims by tenants for loss of personal property due to fire, theft, or acts of God are also common.

NOTE: *A lease will not serve to protect a property owner in every situation. It is quite unlikely that your personal homeowner's insurance policy provides sufficient protection for you as a residential real estate landlord.*

As a property owner contemplating residential house leasing, you should understand the local landlord/tenant laws and requirements in your specific area. Nearly every state now has statutes that serve to protect tenants from devious landlords. Such laws make available minimum standards for *habitability*, minimum *notice* prior to *eviction* of the tenant, and a *joint inspection and inventory* of the property at the start of the lease term.

Property owners can collect a *security deposit*. The deposit is stated as a multiple of the regular monthly rent—often times double. Place the security deposit in an interest-bearing account. The interest must be paid to the tenant at the end of the lease *if* the security deposit is to be returned.

It is also recommended under local *ordinances* (rules) that the rental property have one or more smoke detectors or alarms. Smoke detectors or alarms may further entitle the landlord to a discounted insurance premium.

Example lease provision:

Form 78/94 (Yeo & Lukens) and Form 78C (John C. Clark) provide identical examples of such drafting, reading in pertinent and applicable part:

"This lease does not terminate on the ending date indicated above unless either landlord or tenant give written notice to the other by_____ month _____day_____ year.

_____ days written notice by landlord is required to change any of the terms and conditions of any renewal of this lease.

Renewal length of this lease if not ended by either party as required in [prior paragraph] _____."

A landlord who is eager to repossess a certain residential property from a tenant may opt to notify the tenant, in writing, to remove himself or herself from the residential real property at the *expiration* (conclusion) of the time specified in the notice. The notice may be issued in the following situations:

- at the termination or conclusion of a term of the lease;

- at the forfeiture of the lease for violation or breach of its terms and conditions; or,

- based upon the failure of the tenant upon the landlord's demand to meet and fulfill any rent held in reserve, unpaid, and owing.

LEASES FOR ROOMS OR PORTIONS OF A HOUSE

Inquiries often emerge as to the legal status of the resident of an "apartment hotel" or a lodger in the furnished room of one's private home. Housing arrangements of these individuals often include the sharing of common areas such as a kitchen or bathroom facilities with other residents. Pennsylvania statutes do not clearly provide a general definition of who is a "tenant." *Common law* doctrine and principles must be discussed and reviewed to ascertain whether the law of landlord and tenant will control some of these less common housing arrangements.

PENNSYLVANIA CASES

  📖 The renting of furnished rooms set off in a private house, also occupied by the owner, was found to constitute a lease agreement in one case. (*Davis v. Hartel*, 56 Pa. Super. 557,564 (1914).) The Court gave particular attention to the fact that the rooms were set off from the rest of the house to establish a particular area under control of the *lessee* (tenant).

  📖 In another trial court opinion, the right to exclusive possession of at least part of a room and the fact that the room became the tenant's permanent residence led to the finding that the letting of furnished rooms in a home created a *tenancy*. (*Yost v. Hamilton Apt. Co.*, 33 Montg. Co. 273 (1917).)

OTHER CASE LAW

In determining whether renting a furnished room creates a tenancy, courts look to several factors that indicate whether the occupant has the requisite *exclusive possession* of the premises necessary to establish a tenancy. These factors include:

- the roomer's ability to lock the room door;

- the availability of maid service; and,

- the duration of occupancy.

Courts have found the renting of a furnished room to create lease agreements in many cases:

📖 *Brin v. Sidenstucker*, 232 Iowa 1258,8 N.W. 2d 423, 145 A.L.R. 359 (1943);

📖 *Lambert v. Sine*, 123 Utah 145, 256 P.2d 241 (1953);

📖 *Levesque v. Columbia Hotel*, 141 Me. 393, 44 A.2d 728 (1945);

📖 *State v. Bowman*, 202 Minn. 44, 279 N.W. 214 (1938); and,

📖 *Mathews v. Livingston*, 86 Conn. 263, 85 A. 529 (1912).

The case for the finding of a tenancy becomes particularly strong where the lodger is not a transient *guest*, but uses the room as a permanent residence, as a *home*, for a continuous period of months or years. (*Levesque v. Columbia Hotel*, and *Brin v. Sidenstucker*.)

GENERAL LEASE REQUIREMENTS

All wide-ranging conditions and circumstances should be well thought-out in drafting lease terms.

- the term or period of the lease agreement being issued;

- a start or beginning date;

- an ending or concluding date;

- instructions for terminating the lease relationship:
  - the number of days of notice to be agreed upon to stop or terminate the lease at the ending date. Otherwise, one must include the waiver of notice to stop or terminate the lease at the ending date; and,

- renewal term:
  - automatic or habitual renewal, if any, and the term of such automatic renewal;
  - the number of days of notice required for the landlord to amend or alter the terms and conditions of renewal; or,
  - the number of days of notice to be issued in order to stop or terminate the renewal option or period.

MAKING AND USING LEASE AGREEMENTS 4

Lease agreements are documents that obligate the tenant to a periodic or long-term rental. These agreements also require the tenant to stay for the duration of the contract—usually one year. Unless there are legally extenuating circumstances (nonpayment of rent or the breaking of a lease agreement provision), the landlord cannot change any of the terms until the lease agreement has expired, unless the document stipulates otherwise or the tenant gives written agreement to changes. If a lease agreement extends for a year or longer, it is exempt from the Landlord/Tenant Act, but only if the exemption is approved by the tenant's attorney.

PROS AND CONS OF LEASE AGREEMENTS

Pros. The tenant is protected from rent raises for the duration of the lease agreement. As long as the tenant abides by the terms of the lease agreement, he or she is guaranteed to keep the rental unit for the duration. In addition, there is less likelihood of a future dispute because a written lease agreement states the responsibilities of both parties.

Cons. If the tenant leaves before the term of the lease agreement has expired, the tenant may still be held liable for the rent for the full period. In most states, and in Pennsylvania, the landlord is required to make an earnest effort to find a new renter as soon as possible. If one is found, the tenant is only responsible for the period the unit remains un-rented.

What to Include in the Lease

The lease agreement is the agreement between the landlord and the tenant for renting a property. The lease agreement can be oral (spoken) or in writing. If the tenant does not have a written lease agreement, he or she has an oral lease agreement.

WRITTEN AGREEMENT

Upon executing a written lease agreement to rent, the landlord should be certain the tenant has the following information:

- name of the landlord;

- amount of the rent;

- when the rent is to be paid;

- to whom and where the rent should be paid;

- amount of the security deposit;

- to whom problems and repairs should be referred;

- type of lease agreement—written or oral;

- term of the lease agreement;

- who bears responsibility to pay utilities; and,

- rules and regulations about pets and/or children.

NOTE: *The tenant must make sure that all blanks are filled in or crossed out of the lease agreement and that all changes are made before signing.*

If the tenant has a written lease agreement, every agreement between the tenant and the landlord must be put in the lease agreement including any promises by the landlord to make repairs. Ask for and get a copy of the lease agreement.

Warning: Never sign any lease agreement before reading it carefully. Normally, numbers are applied to each section of a standard lease agreement.

The lease agreement sets forth the obligation that the tenant owes to the landlord and the obligation that the landlord owes to the tenant.

ORAL
AGREEMENT

Upon executing an oral lease agreement to rent, the landlord should be sure to at least state the following information to the tenant:

- who is the tenant and who is the landlord;

- the location being rented;

- the amount of rent due;

- the length of time that the property is being rented (month-to-month or year-to-year): and,

- who pays the utilities.

ADDITIONAL
ITEMS

Smoke detectors are standard features in rental properties within Pennsylvania. It is in keeping with fire safety and fire regulations that all premises for rent maintain smoke detectors in working order. Often, landlords may require proof of fire insurance when leasing a premises. Fire inspections often include an examination of the smoke detection system maintained on the property. A provision in a lease agreement which addresses smoke detectors can be drafted as follows:

Smoke Detectors

The landlord acknowledges that tenant has been instructed by landlord on procedures needed to test the smoke detectors in the Leased Premises and in the building of which the Leased premises is a part of.

The tenant acknowledges that tenant fully understands how to test the smoke detectors.

The tenant promises to test monthly or more frequently, as recommended by the manufacturer, all smoke detectors in and on the leased premises.

(continued)

> The tenant agrees to notify the landlord immediately if any smoke detector is found not working or any reason. tenant agrees to pay for and keep fresh batteries in each smoke detector in the Leased premises.
>
> The tenant agrees to pay any loss or damage incurred by the landlord that results from tenant's failure to comply with any part of paragraph addressing smoke detectors.

RULES AND REGULATIONS

Leases typically include some form of "Rules and Regulations" that serve as restrictions on the tenant's use of the leased property. These restrictions protect the landlord's property as well as the enjoyment of the adjacent property by other tenants. Although not often the subject of analysis in judicial opinion, lease "laws" are frequently a very effectual way of avoiding disorderly or intolerable conduct. They also offer a possible foundation for getting rid of a tenant who persistently breaches the rules to the disadvantage of other tenants.

The purpose of calling these limitations upon conduct as "restrictions" in a particular lease agreement section serves to highlight the importance of the section. While the drafting of rules and regulations must represent the specific needs and conditions of the landlord, the tenant, and the leased premises, some broad issues are usually focused upon in such rules:

- maintenance of leased premises;

- reasonable use of common areas;

- car washing or repair, barbequing or cooking, retail or sales activity, etc.;

- restrictions upon disturbance of neighbors: use of radios, stereos, TVs, etc.;

- storage and use of hazardous materials and waste disposal; or,

- restrictions upon posting signs and advertisements.

Many form leases simply refer to written rules either attached to the lease agreement or available at a designated office. Typically, such forms also provide that all rules must be written and in keeping with the related terms of the lease agreement. Such provisions do not change unless the tenant expressly agrees in writing.

The landlord may set forth certain general rules to be followed by all tenants in a rental unit. Such provisions do not address the relationship between the landlord and the tenant specifically, rather they address the manner in which the tenant must conduct himself or herself when using the premises or when interacting with other tenants. Examples of general rules or provisions contained within a lease agreement for multiple dwelling units are as follows:

Rules

Tenant must comply with landlords rules. Notice of new rules will be (given to tenant, landlord need not enforce rules against other tenants. landlord is not liable to tenant if another tenant violates these rules. tenant receives no rights under these rules.

The comfort or rights of other tenants must not be interfered with. This means that annoying sounds, smells and lights are not allowed.

No one is allowed on the roof. Nothing may be used in, kept in, placed on, or attached to fire escapes, sills, windows or exterior walls of the apartment or in the hallways or other areas.

Smoking is not permitted in elevators. Messengers and trade people must only use service elevators and service entrances. Bicycles are not allowed on passenger elevators. They must be stored in designated areas.

tenant must give landlord keys to all locks. Doors must be locked at all times. Windows must be locked when tenant is out. All to landlord at the end of the term.

Apartment floors must be covered by carpets or rugs. No waterbeds are allowed in the apartment.

(continued)

Dogs, cats, birds or other animals or pets are not allowed in the apartment or building. Feeding them from the apartment, sidewalks, steps, terrace, balcony or public areas is not allowed.

Garbage disposal rules must be followed. Plumbing fixtures and all other property and equipment must be used only for their intended purpose.

Laundry machines, if any, are used at tenant's risk and cost. Instructions must be followed.

Moving furniture, fixtures or equipment must be scheduled with landlord. tenant must not send landlord's employees on personal errands.

Improperly parked cars may be removed without notice at tenant's cost.

Tenant must not allow the cleaning of the windows or other part of the apartment or building from the outside

Tenant will keep the apartment safe and clean, and will not store or bring hazardous or flammable materials into the building or the apartment.

Tenant will not throw anything from the apartment, or hang or shake anything from sidewalks, steps, windows, terraces or balconies.

TYPICAL LEASE PROVISIONS

Normally, numbers are applied to each section of a standard lease agreement. The following are points usually contained in a lease agreement.

- Identify the parties to the agreement. The landlord is called the "party of the first part" and the tenant is called the "party of the second part."

- Identify the property that is being rented, usually by address and/or apartment number.

- State the term of the lease agreement. How long is the tenant obligated to rent? The lease agreement will usually be month-to-month or year-to-year. The tenant may have a one-year agreement in which the rent is paid monthly. In this case, the term is one year.

- Set out the amount of rent that must be paid. It should explain when the rent should be paid and to whom. Sometimes the landlord will provide a penalty charge if the rent is not paid on time.

- Introduce the landlord's rights and the tenant duties. These are the conditions of the lease agreement which must be kept by the tenant.

- Explain that the tenant must keep the property in the same condition as when it was rented. (The tenant is only responsible for damages that he or she caused to the property. He or she is not responsible for damages from natural wear or if the damages were caused by fire, storm, or other disasters not the fault of the tenant.)

- Direct the tenant to keep the property clean.

- Place the responsibility for trash and garbage removal on the tenant. (If the tenant does not remove the trash, the landlord may remove it and charge the tenant twice as much as the actual cost to remove it.)

- Place the cost of utilities (water and electricity) on the tenant, unless it is specifically provided otherwise, in writing, at the end of the lease agreement.

- Provide that the tenant cannot do anything in the rented property which would cause a hazard or which would be contrary to what the landlord's insurance policy permits. (Ask the landlord what the policy permits.)

- Prohibit the tenant from renting the property or any part of it to anyone else.

- State that the tenant may not move out of the property during the term of the lease agreement without the written agreement of the landlord. (This may not be enforceable, especially now that the law permits the tenant to break the Lease Agreement if the landlord refuses to make necessary repairs. There are no penalties.)

- Prohibit the tenant from participating in any unlawful acts or business, or any acts which cause a nuisance in the property.

- Permit the landlord to enter the property at reasonable times to inspect, to make repairs, or to show it to others for renting or buying. (The landlord does not have to inform the tenant before entering, but the landlord cannot use this clause to harass the tenant. The landlord can put up "for rent" or "for sale" signs.)

- Provide that if the tenant removes any of his or her own goods from the property without the written consent of the landlord, those goods will be available for *distraint* for thirty days after removal. *Distraint* is a remedy used by the landlord to get back rent that the tenant owes. The landlord would distraint, or take, the property of the tenant and sell it.

  NOTE: *The courts have found the distraint procedure to be unconstitutional and the landlord is not allowed to take the tenant's property. If the landlord tries to do this, the tenant should see an attorney immediately.*

- State that if the tenant fails to pay the rent or breaks any condition of the lease agreement, the landlord can ask to be paid all the rent due for the whole term and can cancel the remainder of the lease agreement.

- Provide that the landlord can sue to evict the tenant for paying rent late, even if the landlord accepted rent late in the past. The landlord can also sue for the rent due. (Even if the landlord permitted the tenant to break some provisions of the lease agreement in the past, the landlord can later require strict compliance and can evict if the tenant does not obey the lease agreement.)

- Provide that if the tenant files for bankruptcy or becomes bankrupt, the landlord can require that the rent for the full term of the lease agreement be listed as a debt on the bankruptcy petition.

- Set out a *confession of judgment* provision for rent. This clause allows the landlord to enter a judgment for rent against the tenant without a hearing.

   NOTE: *The tenant should see an attorney if he or she receives a notice that judgment has been entered against him or her.*

- Set out a *confession of judgment provision to evict*. This clause allows the landlord to enter a judgment for possession against the tenant without a hearing.

   NOTE: *The tenant should see an attorney if he or she receives notice that a judgment has been entered against him or her.*

- Provide that all agreements must be in writing. (This means that any oral agreements between the landlord and tenant are not enforceable.)

- Automatically renew the lease agreement, with the same provisions in effect, if the tenant stays in the premises past the term stated.

- Set out any additional agreement or changes in the lease agreement. (Unless agreements between the landlord and tenant are in writing, they cannot be enforced.)

- Bind the landlord and tenant to the lease agreement by their signatures. (The tenant should not sign the lease agreement until he or she has read it carefully and understands it fully.)

HOW TO MODIFY THE LEASE TERMS

Lease agreements may be modified if both landlord and tenant agree on the changes. The changes may become effective whenever they wish. If the tenant does not agree to any changes, the landlord or the tenant may wish to terminate (end) the lease agreement.

Change in the lease agreement must be made according to certain requirements. Often, written lease agreements contain a clause explaining how changes in the lease agreement are to be made. Such a clause may state that any changes must be in writing and signed by both the landlord and the tenant. In year-to-year lease agreements, there is often a clause that states changes can be made after giving one month's notice. The lease agreement should be read carefully to see if it contains any clause that states how your lease agreement may be modified.

To change an oral lease agreement or a written lease agreement which does not say how changes are to be made, notice of a change must be given in writing, stating the required change and when it will become effective. All lease agreement modifications should only take place at the beginning of a "new term." This means that, in an oral or month-to-month lease agreement, the landlord must give the tenant the notice at least one full rental period before the change is to take place.

RENT 5

SPECIFIC PROVISIONS TO INCLUDE IN LEASES

Specific provisions or terms that must be addressed in every rental arrangement include each of the following:

- total rental amount payable through the course of the term, where the leasehold exists for a period of years;

- amount of the payment due for each individual period of installments (amount of each monthly payment, for example, if the term of the lease requires a monthly payment);

- stipulation that payment installments be paid on or before the stated due date (for example, on the *first* of the month);

- payment period;

- beginning date of initial payment;

- for a partial period of occupancy, the total rent due will be modified and adjusted on a prorated or reduced basis;

- stipulation that rent be paid without prior notice upon demand from the landlord;

- location to which the tenant is to remit the rental payment;

- supplementary rent, if warranted;

- rent may be accelerated by the landlord as a penalty to the tenant for the tenant's breaches of certain requirements in the lease agreement;

- applicable charges as penalty for late payment;

- *clemency* or grace period; and,

- rent may be waived by the landlord at the landlord's discretion.

SAMPLE CLAUSES

The following are easily read rental clauses or provisions:

Rental Payment

Rental Amount to be paid each month - $ _____ /month.

tenant consents to remit payment of the monthly rental amount due on or before the _____ day of every month hereafter.

Landlord shall not be required to request or to (DEMAND) tenant to remit rental payment.

Tenant consents to remit payment by first class US mail, postage paid, or to deliver same in person to landlord at the location as follows:

State address:

_____

Name

_____

Street

_____

City   State   ZIP

Should tenant post the rent in a US Mailbox to landlord, the payment date will be the date upon which such letter is postmarked.

Further, the requirements which follow below may be additionally added to the hereinabove rental terms should such additions be favored by the signing parties.

Delinquent or Tardy Rent

Landlord's receipt and acceptance (at any time) of a delinquent or late rental payment is not considered to be a waiver of timely payment(s) at a later date.

Tenant concurs and promises to remit a late charge of $ _____ per day if tenant fails to remit the rental payment in a timely and prompt fashion.

Modification of Rental Payment for Incomplete Occupancy

If this Lease Agreement commences after the _____ day of the month, the first rental payment shall be due and owing upon the execution and signing of the lease. Such limited rental payment due and owing at that point is $ _____.

Supplementary Rental Payment

The landlord may require the tenant to pay for other charges in addition to the rental payment if the tenant's non-compliance with this lease agreement causes damage to the property or creates costs or expenses to the landlord. Regardless of whether such charges are expressed as "rent", they shall be viewed and determined to be "added rent."

Added rental payments shall be assessed and such is payable as rent with the regular rent due at the next payment period.

If the tenant does not pay the additional "rent" in a timely fashion, the landlord shall have the same right(s) against the tenant as if the tenant did not pay rent. It is also advised that the provision

(continued)

or clause be addended as a separate paragraph to the "Additional (Added) Rent" section of the lease to avoid noncompliance with the short paragraph guidelines previously mentioned. Lastly, the lease designer should think about highlighting such a provision or clause by bolding or enlarged typeface because the provision is inclined to expand upon the responsibilities of the tenant.

ACCELERATION PROVISION

The lease may make available the *acceleration* (mandatory pre-payment of rent and charges) of the rental payment upon the failure of the tenant to pay rent or upon the violation or breach of any other promise. A simply worded example of an acceleration provision is as follows:

Tenant is in breach of this lease if tenant fails to make rental payments when due or fails to comply with any other provision of this lease. If tenant breaches this lease:

(a) Tenant must immediately pay all rents for the balance of the term of this lease and landlord may sue for this rent.

Rental payment acceleration clauses have been held to be legal in Pennsylvania.

📖 The landlord's only remedy in a situation in which the lease agreement does not contain an acceleration provision is to evict or eject the tenant. The landlord may claim damages for the tenant's delayed rental payment and any expenses associated with the lawsuit. However, the landlord may not cause a judgment to be entered for future rental payments after the tenant has vacated (left) the property or rental unit. (*Pierce v. Hoffstot*, 211 Pa. Super. Ct. 380, 383, 236 A.2d 828 (1967).)

A situation in which a lease agreement contains no acceleration provision, however, offers only an agreeable action in *ejectment* (or *eviction*) with judgment for damages for delay and expenses. The landlord may not cause a judgment to be entered for future rental payments after the tenant has relinquished his or her residency in the property. (*Wood v. Hollinger*, 9 Chest. 231 (1960).)

LANDLORD'S DEMAND NOTICE

A landlord demand notice is used to notify the tenant in the form of a written notice from a landlord to a tenant who has failed to make rent payments.

This "letter" is frequently referred to as a NOTICE TO QUIT. NOTICE TO QUIT may be used with either a commercial or residential tenant. The document is typically a written communication to the tenant that the rent is past due.

Regulations in Pennsylvania require that this procedure be followed. Thus, it is usually necessary for a landlord to notify a tenant in writing that he or she must give up the premises due to failure to pay rent. Even if a NOTICE TO QUIT is not specifically necessary, it is at all times worthwhile to provide one to the tenant. The written demand notice or NOTICE TO QUIT functions as a critical prompt to the tenant of his or her responsibilities under the lease agreement. It also underscores that leaving the premises does not relieve the tenant of the requirement to make rent payments due under the terms of the lease agreement. If a tenant declines to vacate the premises, a demand notice or NOTICE TO QUIT is regularly essential before a landlord can pursue a tenant *eviction* proceeding in court.

If there is a written lease agreement, it is imperative to assess it first to make certain that all of the necessary notices have been prearranged and set forth as mandatory under the lease agreement. A landlord should take great concern in sending the NOTICE TO QUIT by the method required by local law. Usually this is certified mail with return receipt requested.

Should the tenant not vacate the premises under the demand notice or NOTICE TO QUIT, a lawsuit is frequently essential to compel eviction of the tenant. You should seek the services of an attorney if you need to file a lawsuit for eviction.

SECURITY DEPOSITS 6

IMPORTANT MATTERS TO ADDRESS IN THE LEASE

The security deposit provision must be well-crafted and must speak to numerous important matters including each one of the following:

- essential agreement of the parties that the security deposit must serve not only as a promise against damages to the leased property, but also must serve as a guarantee against breach of any lease agreement provision, such as timely rental payments;

- amount of the deposit and the way in which the amount is to be calculated;

- method by which such deposit shall be held (usually in an escrow account to remain in the custody of the landlord);

- circumstances to facilitate the return of the security deposit to tenant including:
  - inspection of property by the landlord, and
  - vacation of property;

- fulfillment of all terms of the lease agreement by the tenant;

- deposit for damages caused or actual losses and costs to repair;

- circumstances under which liability of the tenant or landlord is established for injuries suffered upon the property which exceed the amount of the security deposit; and,

- in accordance with Pennsylvania statutory requirement, how much interest shall be paid after two years of occupancy of the tenant.

ESTABLISHING A DEPOSIT AMOUNT

As established in Pennsylvania statutes, the sum of the security deposit that can be held by a landlord is restricted. For the first year, no landlord may require an amount to exceed two months of rent to be deposited in an escrow account for the payment of damages to the leased premises.

During the second year and in subsequent years of the lease, or during any renewal of the original lease agreement, the sum required to be deposited cannot exceed one month of rent.

During the third year or subsequent year of a lease, or during any renewal after the expiration of two years of tenancy, the landlord can require one month of rent. At the termination of the lease or upon surrender and acceptance of the premises, the escrow funds (along with the interest) will be returned to the tenant. (PA Stat., Sections 511.2 and 512.)

If a tenant has been in possession of the premises for a period of five years or longer, any increase or increases in rent shall not require an increase in the security deposit.

Thus, where the situation warrants such handling, the lease agreement may be composed to make available not only a security deposit of two months of rent, but also include a payment of the last month of rental payment as well.

Whenever a situation in which the period of the lease goes beyond one year, the lease agreement must speak to the intended mandate of the Landlord/Tenant Act which designates that where the lease term lengthens into a second year, the security deposit must be reduced in an amount equal to one month of rent.

The security deposit may not be increased by the landlord after the tenant has resided in the premises continuously for a period of five years. Pennsylvania Statutes indicate that the five year period does not necessarily have to be set forth in a "five-year" term lease but may occur as a result of the tenant's occupancy for separate smaller lease terms equaling five years in total.

SPECIAL CONSIDERATIONS

ESCROW ACCOUNT

For security deposits that exceed $100.00, the landlord must establish a bank escrow account for the deposit. The landlord must notify the tenant in writing of the name and address of the bank in which his or her escrow is held.

Landlord will deposit the security deposit at [name of bank]:_____

Tenant must vacate the Leased Premises and submit new address to landlord to be eligible for return of the security deposit.

INTEREST-BEARING ACCOUNT

After the second year, the landlord must retain the security deposit in an interest-bearing account. When the landlord makes use of an interest-bearing account, the landlord can retain one percent per year of the amount of the security deposit. The landlord must pay the tenant all other interest once a year.

The tenant cannot use the security deposit to pay rent without the written approval of the landlord. The landlord may make use of the security deposit for unpaid rental payments and damages which are the tenant's responsibility—excluding normal wear and tear.

The deposits held by the landlord for less than two years need not earn interest payable to the tenant. However, after the second year of the lease, the landlord must make a provision for the tenant's funds to be deposited in an account bearing interest. (PA Stat., Title 68, Sec. 250.511 b.)

RETURNING THE SECURITY DEPOSIT

RETURN OF
SECURITY
DEPOSIT

Within thirty days after the termination of the lease agreement, the landlord must provide the tenant with a written list of any damages to the premise and a full accounting of any rent due. The landlord must deliver to the tenant the balance of any security deposit and interest thereupon, if any, remaining after deducting such sums as needed to recoup the damages to the premises or for unpaid rent. If the tenant does not provide the required forwarding address, it will prevent the landlord from being required to return the deposit. (*Shoemaker v. Henry*, 35 D.& C. 3d 206 (C.C.P. Adams 1984).)

📖 Nevertheless, the mere appearance of the forwarding address upon the envelope of the letter of notification to the landlord of the tenant's objective to vacate the property is deemed sufficient as compliance with this statutory requirement. (*Adamsky v. Picknick*, 412 Pa. Super. 544, 603 A.2d 1069 (1992).)

Security Deposit

Tenant has compensated landlord with a security deposit of $_____as a protection that said tenant will carry out his/her requirements as set forth in the terms and under this lease Agreement. Landlord can make use of said security deposit to recompense for damages caused as a result of breach of this Leas by tenant. Further, landlord can make use of said security deposit to recompense for damages to the Leased Premises. Tenant must compensate for damages which are not sheltered by the security deposit as added rent. Tenant cannot make use of the security deposit as rental payment for the Leased Premises. Landlord can retain security deposit should tenant fail to remit rental payments or should tenant vacate prior to the conclusion of the lease period.

To get the security deposit returned, the tenant must give the landlord, or his or her agent, a forwarding address in writing at or before the time the tenant actually moves out. The landlord must then, within thirty days from the date the tenant moves out:

● return the security deposit, or

● send the tenant a list of damages the tenant caused in the apartment, the cost of the repairs, plus any extra money left over from the security deposit.

SECURITY
DEPOSIT NOT
RETURNED

If the landlord does not return the security deposit or does not provide the written list of damages within thirty days, the tenant can sue the landlord for double the security deposit by going to a district justice's office and filing a complaint against the landlord.

After the second anniversary of the lease agreement the tenant is entitled to receive on a yearly basis interest on all funds over $100 deposited by the landlord in an interest-bearing account. The landlord is entitled to receive as administrative expenses a sum equivalent to one per cent annum upon the security deposit.

The law states that any landlord who fails to provide a written list within thirty days shall give up all rights to keep any part of the money held as a security deposit. (68 P.S. Sec. 250.512.)

REPAIRS

WHO IS RESPONSIBLE FOR REPAIRS

Lease agreements should state who is responsible for different kinds of repairs. For example, the tenant who is renting a house, rather than an apartment, may have a lease that states that all minor repairs are the responsibility of the tenant and all major repairs are the responsibility of the landlord.

If the tenant has an oral lease agreement, or a written lease agreement that does not state who is responsible for repairs, the general rule is that the landlord is responsible for all major repairs and repairs necessary because of normal wear and tear. If the tenant caused the damage, the tenant may be responsible for repairing the damage. For example, if the tenant's child breaks a window, the tenant may have to repair it.

When repairs are required, the tenant should inform the landlord of the needed repairs. This information should be provided in writing, and the tenant should provide to the landlord a fair chance to make the repairs. If the tenant has difficulty in getting the landlord to make the repairs, there are several actions which the tenant can undertake.

- Call the Bureau of Codes Enforcement and request a housing code inspection.

- Terminate the Lease Agreement and move out.

● Arrange to have the repairs made himself or herself by a reputable repair person and deduct the cost from the rent.

NOTE: *This procedure can be dangerous if done without the landlord's agreement.*

● Recent new law in Pennsylvania now allows the tenant to stop paying some or all rent if the landlord does not make necessary repairs. The tenant who withholds rent when the landlord has failed to make necessary repairs may have a good defense if the landlord decides to sue for delinquent rent or eviction, if he or she can prove that the house or apartment is worth only the smaller amount of rent. This new law is called *implied warranty of habitability* and gives tenants more rights than the former law did.

Pennsylvania law allows the tenant to make necessary repairs and deduct the cost of the repairs from the rent under certain circumstances. Under the former law, repair and deduct was allowed in only two situations:

• the landlord had promised to make repairs but repeatedly failed or neglected to do so, or

• the repair was necessary to prevent further injury to the property.

The old repair and deduct remedy could result in eviction based on non-payment of rent. To avoid eviction for non-payment of rent, the tenant had to show that the landlord consented to the repair. The best protection for the tenant was to get a signed agreement from the landlord authorizing the tenant to make the repair. Then, when the repair was made, the tenant paid the balance of the rent with a copy of a receipt for the repairs. The cost of the repair had to be reasonable and receipts were absolutely necessary.

If the tenant failed to get the consent of the landlord, the landlord could decide to terminate the lease agreement and evict the tenant.

It is important that the tenant inform the landlord in writing of his or her intention to stop paying all or part of the rent if necessary repairs are not made in a reasonable amount of time. The tenant should keep a copy of the letter and copies of all receipts for repairs. If the landlord decides to sue the tenant for that portion of the rent which was withheld, the tenant will need these records as part of his or her defense.

The landlord is permitted to enter the premises at reasonable times (normally daylight hours) for the purpose of inspection or to make repairs and should first notify the tenant.

The landlord is permitted to make rules and regulations after the lease agreement goes into effect. However, these rules and regulations may deal only with the health of the tenants and the safety of the premises.

SUBLETTING AND ASSIGNMENTS 8

AGREEMENT TO SUBLET

An agreement to sublet or a SUBLEASE AGREEMENT is used by a residential tenant to *let out* or *sublease* a portion of his or her remaining lease term.

An agreement to sublet is used to sublease the tenant's dwelling to someone else for a part of the remaining lease term. Usually, work requirements or an extended vacation means that the tenant will relocate for an extended period, but will return to his or her home. In such cases, the tenant is required to pay rent to the landlord for the vacant residence, unless the premises has been subleased.

All agreements involving an interest in real estate should be made in writing. The law requires that any such agreement must be in writing to be enforceable. Thus, a written sublease protects both parties.

Residential leases provide that the original tenant cannot assign or sublease the property unless the landlord consents to such an arrangement. A landlord will probably want to examine the sublease agreement prior to offering consent.

The law does not generally require a landlord to approve a request to sublease. A great deal in these circumstances depends upon the way in which the matter is addressed. The landlord will likely not give final approval until the proposed subtenant is identified and until he or she is presented with a written sublease. The landlord will evaluate the subtenant in much the same way he or she would evaluate a new tenant.

ASSIGNMENT

Assignment of a lease is different than a sublease. In assignment, all of the leased property for the remainder of the leased term is transferred to a new party. The original tenant vacates completely, and the new tenant takes over absolutely. The new tenant, as an *assignee*, pays rent directly to the landlord.

In a sublease, the original tenant will return to the leased premises prior to his or her lease term is ended. The original tenant also continues to be liable on the lease, including, but not limited to, making monthly rental and other required payments to the landlord. To offset this obligation, the tenant collects rent from the subtenant. As a consequence, the original tenant becomes the "landlord" of the subtenant.

PERSONAL
PROPERTY AND
FURNITURE

Tenants often find it necessary or practical to leave their furniture to be used by the subtenant. Thus, the sublease should include statements requiring the subtenant to take care of and be responsible for these things. If furniture is left for the subtenant, it is a good idea to get renter's insurance to cover these items. Inform the insurance agent that a subletting arrangement is in place and that the subtenant's use of these items of property does not invalidate the insurance coverage.

ASSIGNMENT OF LEASE AGREEMENT BY THE TENANT

The tenant's assignment of the lease agreement allows a tenant or assignor in a real estate lease, either commercial or residential, to *assign* his or her interest to another party called the *assignee*. Contract law commonly instructs that a party holding an interest in an agreement may assign such interest to another person as long as that agreement does not prohibit such assignment. If the agreement prohibits the assignment, then assignment can still be made if the other party gives consent.

Frequently, the tenant desires to assign because he or she has found larger or more desirable premises somewhere else. Thus, if early termination of the lease agreement is not allowable, the tenant may assign its interest as an adjustment to the landlord and to reduce the weight of monthly rent payments.

NOTE: *The assignor (original tenant) should be careful in selecting the new tenant. Assignment does not release the original tenant of his or her obligations under the agreement. Therefore, if the assignee, or new tenant, fails to pay lease payments in a timely manner, the landlord may collect from the assignor.*

Since the original tenant assigns rights to deposits and other payments, it may be suitable for the assignee to make a payment to the assignor.

Numerous leases provide that the tenant cannot assign unless the landlord first consents. While a tenant may have successfully negotiated an assignment with another individual, it is also imperative to evaluate the lease agreement to make certain that assignment is allowable. If assignment is not permitted, the tenant should tell his or her desires to the landlord prior to proceeding.

The assignor should take care to get the landlord's consent prior to making any legally binding preparations and provisions with the assignee. If the assignor and assignee make a bargain, and the landlord declines to consent, the assignor may be subject to a claim of breach of contract from the prospective assignee.

The broad restrictions of an assignment section in a lease agreement should address the following:

The lease agreement shall be binding upon heirs, administrators, executors, successors, and assigns of landlord and tenant. If assignment or subletting is permitted, conditions may include:

- expressly written consent of the landlord is required to assign or sublet;

- consent shall not be unreasonably withheld;

- consent of the landlord in a single event does not create an ongoing waiver of right to withhold consent in the future; and,

- remedy for violation of the conditions—termination of the lease agreement.

Again, the legal difference between an assignment and sublease is that assignment occurs when the tenant transfers the whole leased premises to another. Subletting is the transfer of only a part of the tenant's rights to the premises. Regardless of this mechanical difference, cases commonly use these interchangeably, and for purposes of this book they are treated similarly.

📖 Where a lease stipulates, however, that an assignment without the consent of the landlord is prohibited, *any* assignment is ineffective. (*Girard Trust Co. v. Cosgrove*, 270 Pa. 570, 113 A. 741 (1921). *B.C. & H. Corp. v. Acme Markets. Inc.*, 19 D.&C.3d 419 (Somerset 1980); *Martens v. McGinnis*, 45 Lack. Jur. 117 (1944).)

📖 Provisions in lease agreements that limit assignment are generally not favored and so are strictly construed against the landlord. (*Regenbogen v. Security Trust Co. of Potts town*, 75 York 41 (1961).

📖 In the absence of a provision to the contrary, lease restrictions on assignments will be construed as exposing the tenant to damages for a breach, and not as conditions making the assignment *void* or resulting in a *forfeiture*. (*Wahl v. M. F. Land Co.*, 30 Som. 291 (1975).)

NOTE: *Carefully consider whether assignment is to be permitted, and if so, which conditions will be necessary to allow assignment. Careful drafting of this provision will protect the intentions of both parties.*

Subleasing and Assignment Provisions

This Lease Agreement shall be binding upon the respective heirs, executors, administrators, successors and assigns of the parties. The tenant will not assign this lease or sublet the Leased premises, or any part of premises without the prior written consent of landlord. Landlord will not unreasonably withhold this consent.

Continued Responsibility to the Tenant

Tenant must not assign all or part of this lease, or sublet all or part of the apartment, or permit any other person to use the apartment. tenant must get landlord's written permission each time tenant wants to assign or sublet. Permission to assign or sublet is good only for that assignment or subLease. tenant remains bound to the terms of this lease after an assignment or sublet is permitted, even if landlord accepts money from the new assignee or subtenant. The amount accepted will be credited against money due from tenant, as landlord shall determine. The assignee or subtenant does not become landlord's tenant. tenant is responsible for acts and neglect of any person in the apartment including a new assignee or subtenant.

ENDING A LEASE EARLY 9

CANCELLATION OR TERMINATION

A method by which premature or early termination may be accomplished and the scope of which that termination is supported should be declared expressly in the written lease. The most important feature of such a provision is the type of notice that is to be presented to the parties.

In a situation where a party does not comply with notice requirements, or the *lessee* (tenant) has not *waived* (given up) notice requirements, a landlord may fail in his or her action to regain possession of the property.

📖 The Pennsylvania case law concerning appropriate notice is characteristically associated with ejectment, removal, or eviction based upon a breach of a required term or condition rather than termination before the expiration of the period or term. (*Patrycia Brothers. Inc. v. McKeefrey*, 38 D.& C.2d 149, 53 Del. Co. 409 (1966).)

Termination of Lease by Either Landlord or Tenant.

The landlord or the tenant may terminate the lease prior to the term stated in the disputed paragraph by issuing to the other party at least thirty (30) days an expressly written notice of the desire or intent to conclude the lease.

Termination may be desired in certain specific instances that are not commonly accounted for within leases. The Restatement (Second) of Property recognizes a tenancy terminable at the option of one of the parties to the lease upon the occurrence of a specific event. (Such a tenancy is called a *term of years subject to a condition subsequent.*) Section 1.7, comment "e" of the Pennsylvania Restatement (Second) of Property has also recognized termination by a *subsequent condition.* (*Girard Trust Co. v. Raiguel*, 93 Pa. Super. 123 (1928).) The function of these certain provisions may help the landlord or the tenant.

Example: Sometimes the landlord tries to provide for a termination of the lease upon the sale of the premises, should such a provision make the premises more marketable for sale as in a single-family home rental.

Such provisions may similarly apply to the advantage of the tenant, such as the following two examples:

Tenant Employment Transfer Clause

If the tenant's employer transfers the tenant to a new employment location more than 50 miles from the Leased property, the tenant may terminate this lease prior to the end of the term stated in the paragraph. Prior to terminating this lease under this provision, tenant must:

(continued)

1. Give the landlord written notice of the tenant's intent to conclude this lease at least 30 days before tenant intends to end this lease;

2. Give the landlord written proof from the tenant's employer showing the transfer;

3. Pay the landlord an early end-of-lease charge in the amount of two months' rent.

The lease will terminate under this provision upon the last day of the calendar month which follows the end of the 30 day notice period.

Death Clause

If one of the tenants residing within the leased property dies, the surviving spouse may terminate this lease prior to the end of the term stated in the paragraph. Prior to ending this lease under this provision, the surviving spouse must:

1. Give the landlord written notice of the tenant's intent to conclude this lease at least 30 days before the surviving spouse intends to end this lease;

2. Pay the landlord a premature end of lease charge in the amount of two (2) months' rent.

The lease will terminate under this provision upon the last day of the calendar month which follows the end of the 30 day notice period. The provision provided above addressing termination by death may be broadened or extended to afford for termination upon the unexpected incapacitation or physical disability of the tenant, provided that incapacitation is authenticated expressly in writing to landlord by a certified physician or by some further similar evidence.

TERMINATING A MONTH-TO-MONTH TENANCY

In the Commonwealth of Pennsylvania, a tenant occupying a property absent a written lease, or one occupying the property after the term of the written lease has run out or expired, is called a *month-to-month tenant*. The LANDLORD'S NOTICE TO TERMINATE TENANCY is a letter from a landlord terminating a tenant's month-to month tenancy. Written notice of a termination of the month-to-month tenancy is always legally mandatory.

Generally, the notice should be given at least thirty days before the termination date. This time frame both satisfies the district justice court requirements and provides a reasonable time for the tenant to vacate.

The method of providing the notice is also important. The delivery of the notice must comply with both the lease and with local law. Personal delivery of the notice is effective in Pennsylvania. However, posting the notice on the premises and sending the notice by certified mail, return receipt requested is the method preferred by the courts. It is recommended that delivery take place by at least two methods—one definitely being certified mail, the other being personal delivery by a competent person over eighteen years of age.

TERMINATING A WRITTEN LEASE AGREEMENT

A LETTER OF TERMINATION OF LEASE AGREEMENT is used by a landlord and tenant who desire to terminate the lease prior to the conclusion of the term. From time to time, a long-standing tenant must relocate or has outgrown the leased premises. A tenant may desire to travel to another location, and the landlord may have a more suitable replacement tenant already waiting. Landlords may wish to terminate a lease to make room for another tenant.

It is always recommended that the landlord and the tenant put their pact to terminate the lease agreement in writing. If they fail to do so, a successor to the landlord may attempt to collect rent from the tenant assuming the rent is overdue. Often, the tenant will be required to pay a specific sum to the landlord to terminate the lease agreement early. This is an accepted drafting provision and protects the landlord form premature departures by the tenant.

TAKING BACK THE PROPERTY THROUGH EJECTMENT

The landlord may be at liberty to retake possession of the leased premises either by reason of breach of the lease agreement term or due to the fact that the lease period has expired. The landlord can uphold an *ejectment* action as set forth in the statute. (PA. Stat., Title 68, Sec. 250.501.) The accessibility of an ejectment action is based upon the entitlement of the landlord to take back the real property. In creating a lease agreement, the landlord should be careful to keep the option to retake control of the premises based upon breach of the lease agreement. Commonly, ejectment can occur with an all-encompassing provision permitting the landlord to end the lease agreement and retake possession of the premises upon non-payment of rent.

A difference exists between a "covenant" and a "condition" as drafted in a lease agreement. The "covenant" is a promise to act, or to refrain from acting in a certain manner. The "condition" creates a possessory interest in the property and, as a result, any breach or violation of the "condition" may result in the forfeiture of the tenant's interest in the property. The breach or violation of the "covenant" does not cause a forfeiture of the tenant's interest in the property and thus the remedy to the landlord for the tenant's breach of a "covenant" can be money damages, while the breach of a "condition" by the tenant can result in the tenant being compelled to surrender or give up the lease. (*Williams v. Notopolis*, 259 Pa. 469, 103 A. 290 (1918).)

PROBLEMS WITH THE TENANCY 10

INABILITY TO GIVE POSSESSION

A clause should be placed in the lease agreement to address such instances in which the landlord is unable to give possession to the tenant on the date indicated. Nevertheless, the landlord should be sure to make provision for the odds and plainly set forth the rights of both the landlord and the tenant should an occurrence such as this manifest itself. When drafting such clauses, the landlord should consider a number of factors.

In circumstances where possession cannot be agreed:

- begin term of lease, but suspend rental payment until the tenant obtains possession, or

- delay beginning of the lease term until the tenant has possession.

If inability to give possession is not caused by the landlord:

- hold the landlord harmless for liability for damages, and

- draft a provision to include rent waiver for the period of the tenant's non-occupancy since the tenant has the right to occupy the premises, and the tenant has not been able to gain access.

DELAY OF
POSSESSION

It is beneficial for the landlord to address in drafting the lease agreement any possibility that he or she may not be able to give possession of the leased premises to the tenant. The landlord should be certain to address the rights of both the landlord and the tenant in the section dealing with inability to give possession just in case such an event occurs. The tenant's response should be limited to the termination of the lease after a specified period, provided that possession is not given within that specified time. The tenant should recover any consideration paid, as well as all prepaid rent, security deposit and other charges.

The main circumstances that cause the landlord to be unable to provide possession of the premises to the tenant are:

- hold-over of a previous tenant;

- damage to the property which makes it unsuitable for habitation; or,

- need for wide-ranging maintenance.

FAILURE TO
GIVE
POSSESSION

If the landlord is unable to give the tenant possession of the property at the beginning of the lease term, for any reason not caused by the tenant, the tenant shall have the choice of:

1. ending this lease and recovering rent and security deposit (without charge or interest) and any other money already paid, or

2. delaying the beginning of the lease term until the landlord is able to give possession.

No rent will be due until possession is available. If the tenant delays the lease term, the tenant may end this lease at any time before the landlord gives possession. The landlord is not liable for damages where the failure to deliver possession is due to conditions beyond the landlord's control.

The landlord shall not be responsible if he or she cannot provide the tenant possession on the beginning date of the term. rent starts at the beginning of the term unless the landlord cannot give possession (rent shall then be payable when possession is available). Landlord must give possession within a reasonable time, or else tenant may cancel and obtain a refund of money deposited. The landlord will notify the tenant when possession is available. The conclusion date of the lease will not be changed.

DESTRUCTION OF PREMISES

The destruction provision must address the following aspects:

- prompt notice to the landlord of any dangerous condition that threatens the leased premises;

- total destruction of the leased premises;

- on-time notice to the landlord of destruction;

- restriction upon continuous occupancy; and,

- return of advanced rent payments and security deposit.

The likelihood of the destruction of the leased premises must be considered in the lease agreement. According to Pennsylvania law, absent a provision that places the hazard or burden of loss upon a party named in the lease agreement, the tenant (generally) is held harmless and released from contractual obligations when his or her intent to use the property for a specific purpose is frustrated by accidental destruction of the property. (Albert M. Greenfield & Co.. Inc. v. Kolea, 475 Pa. 351, 380 A.2d 758 (1977).)

The degree of "destruction" becomes the focus of this issue. While the Pennsylvania Supreme Court in the above case intended to suggest total destruction was essential, the tenant should not bear the risk in the "event of total destruction of the building."

The landlord and tenant may elect to agree to a variety of solutions to the issue of a damaged leased premises. The lease may simply order extinction of the lease agreement in the occurrence of total destruction. A lease may, in the alternative, provide that the lease agreement can be terminated where the premises has been so spoiled that it cannot be restored within a "reasonable time" or within an acknowledged period.

DAMAGE OF
PREMISES

The tenant will notify the landlord without delay if the structure is damaged or spoiled. If the damages are to an extent that the leased premises is partially or completely unlivable:

- the tenant may vacate without delay within 24 hours, and make notification to the landlord that the lease agreement is terminated;

- where continued occupancy is permitted by Pennsylvania law, the tenant may elect to continue to occupy that portion of the leased premises still usable, with a reduction in the tenant's rent by the proportionate damage amount and until the structure is restored;

- in cases where the lease is terminated, the landlord will return all prepaid rental payments plus the security deposit. The amount of prepaid rental payments to be returned shall be calculated as of the date of the loss or damage; and,

- the landlord and the tenant will remain responsible for their own negligence and the negligence of their guests in or on the premises.

LANDLORD'S REMEDIES IF TENANT BREACHES

Some of the ways a tenant may *breach* (break or sever) conditions of the lease agreement are:

- failure to make rental payment or other charges when due and owing;

- violation or failure to perform any covenant or condition of the lease agreement;

- abandonment of the leased property; or,

- bankruptcy of the tenant.

The landlord's remedy to all or any of the above breach conditions is ejectment (eviction).

As with any clauses placed into a lease agreement, the main goal of the parties is that the provisions will be held to be enforceable. It is likely that any problematic provision(s) will be disregarded in entirety rather than being interpreted or rewritten by the judge.

The provisions of a lease dealing with the remedies available to a landlord for a breach by the tenant are, as might be imagined, the most important provisions when it comes to protecting the interests of the landlord. In negotiating a lease, every landlord should be certain that the lease contains those clauses that set forth the landlord's remedies. However, in light of the importance of these clauses, the landlord must be careful not to include unenforceable provisions that could ultimately cause the entire clause to be thrown out by a judge. Therefore, a basic understanding of the law, as it pertains to the most common remedies available to the landlord is important.

The following is an example of the landlord remedies clauses appearing in new plain language lease forms:

Landlord's Actions to Cure

The landlord can file an action to remove the tenant from the Premises in concurrence with applicable laws if the tenant has failed to make rental payments or to submit related lease obligations, only if the landlord has issued to the tenant a five (5) day written notification to quit based upon his/her failure to remit rental payment. At that juncture the lease Agreement is terminated. The complaint for eviction can be filed on the sixth (6th) day. Hearing to address the landlord's complaint for eviction cannot be made until twenty-five (25) days subsequent to the conclusion of the five (5) day notification.

(continued)

Should the tenant fail to execute his/her responsibilities as set forth in the Lease Agreement supplementary to the rental payment, the landlord will issue to the tenant an expressly written notification advising the tenant of the character of the offensive behavior. The landlord must issue to the tenant five (5) days to cease such behavior. Should the intolerable actions continue within the five (5) days or should it reoccur prior to the concluding date of the Lease Agreement, the landlord can issue to the tenant a five (5) day Lease Agreement termination notice made in writing. A complaint for eviction can be filed at the end of this second five (5) day period. Hearing upon the landlord's complaint in eviction cannot be made until twenty (20) days subsequent to conclusion of the second notice.

Remedies afforded the landlord as above-stated are not the landlord's distinct remedies. Other actions are available to the landlord to collect rent, charges, or any other money that landlord is owed under this Lease Agreement.

As allowed by Pennsylvania statute, the above provision reduces the notice periods. Thus, it is recommended that notification of any waiver of rights be *appended* to the above illustrations. The tenant may waive a right to receive a lengthier notice period to *vacate* (leave) the property by a written provision that specifically addresses that notice is being waived.

LANDLORD'S ESCAPE FROM LIABILITY

Provisions can be placed in the lease agreement to release the landlord from liability:

- for acts of landlord, his/her agents or employees due to negligence or other acts;

- for injuries to third parties; or,

- for damage to persons or property for any reason.

A release or *exculpatory* clause in a lease agreement is one that frees the landlord from liability for acting, failing to perform an act, or for an occurrence at the leased property that results in injury or harm to the tenant, to the property of the tenant, or to third parties.

Release/Exculpatory Clause

Both the landlord and the tenant shall be responsible for their own negligence and for the negligence of their guests, family, or third parties whom they permit into, in, or on the Leased premises.

NOTE: *Release clauses that broaden to injuries sustained by others than the tenant, have been subjected to criticism in the courts of Pennsylvania. They have not yet ruled that third parties not part of the lease are not bound by the terms of the release clause. Third parties may be held to the release clause.*

Release of Landlord

The landlord is not liable for injury, property damage, and/ or loss to tenant or guests of tenant.

I, _____,

the tenant releases the landlord from liability for damage, loss, and/or injury caused by other person(s) inhabiting the premises, or by landlord, or his or her agents, or employees. The tenant releases the landlord for losses and/or damages that may result from any of the acts of the tenant and/or omission to act. Thus, each, every, and all claims against the landlord for damage, loss, and/or injury is/are expressly waived by the tenant.

In the case in which injury or damage to any person or personal items in the rental premises, the tenant does hereby:

Releases the landlord from liability, and

Agrees to compensate for loss or claim in any portion of the rental premises unless such injury or damage comes as a result of the carelessness of the landlord.

STANDARD FORM LEASE AGREEMENTS 11

The majority of residential tenants who have entered into a lease agreement have executed some variety of a standard form lease. Such forms are seldom the result of any "negotiating" between the parties. Before a tenant inquires about a possible rental option, the landlord will have previously decided whether an oral or written lease will be used, and as to which form of lease the tenant will sign. Large multi-family buildings and rental complexes are most affected by this standardized lease agreement where the exercise of a specific customary form lease agreement will be non-negotiable.

The parties may in fact discuss a small number of terms, mainly the amount of the rental payments and the period of the lease term. The balance of the form includes abundant fine-print clauses that work against the tenant and in favor of the landlord. Form leases are actually mere *contracts of adhesion* in which the tenant *adheres* to a document that he or she is powerless to alter, having no alternative other than to reject the entire transaction. The Supreme Court of Pennsylvania and the federal courts have continually recognized that form lease provisions do not embody the anticipated terms of a lease agreement freely entered into by the landlord and tenant:

> 📖 Since all form leases contain similar clauses that operate harshly against the tenant and in favor of the landlord—landlords are unwilling to strike the clauses that favor them. It is fruitless for the

prospective tenant of any apartment to seek out a lease without the unfavorable clauses. The result is that the tenant has no bargaining power and must accept the landlord's "terms." (*Galligan v. Arovitch*, 421 Pa. 301,219 A.2d 463, 465 (1966).)

📖 It should be noted further that small type grossly disproportionate to that used in the rest of a contract cannot be ignored. It has its place in law, and, where space is at a premium, it allows for instructions, guidance, and protection which might otherwise be lost. Where it is used to conceal legalistic information that strikes down other rights agreed upon, the courts will look closely to ascertain the true meaning, which may go beyond the legal impact. (*Cutler Corporation v. Latshaw*, 374 Pa. 1, 7,97 A.2d 234 (1953).)

📖 The court may *refuse* to enforce the terms of a printed form contract that is too one sided and too uniformly harsh to one party. (*Campbell Soup Co. v. Wentz*, 172 F .2d 80, 83 (3rd Cir. 1948).)

LANDLORD'S UNDERSTANDING OF TENANT PROTECTIONS

Tenants gain advantage from legal protections under many common law doctrines, as well as under Pennsylvania statutory and United States Constitutional provisions. The common law *warranty of habitability*, implied in residential leases, establishes the landlord's maintenance obligations. Pennsylvania statutes set forth protection for tenants implicated in eviction proceedings. The United States Constitution prohibits discrimination based upon race, color, religion, sex, or national origin. Therefore, no prospective tenant may be denied rental accommodation based solely upon these Constitutionally protected characteristics.

Lease agreement forms include many provisions that establish the tenant *agreed* to waive or give up, certain rights under common law, Pennsylvania statutes, and the Constitution. A classic lease form operates to put forth clauses that stipulate (or bargain away) all of the key legal rights of the tenant.

📖 A legal right can be waived by form contract language only upon a showing that there has been an intentional and voluntary waiver of a known right. (*Transatlantic Consumer Discount Co. v. Kefauver*, 244 Pa. Super. 475, 307 A.2d 303 (1973).)

THE USE OF FORM LEASES AS AN UNFAIR TRADE PRACTICE

The Pennsylvania legislature, in 1968, enacted the Unfair Trade Practice and Consumer Protection Law. (Pennsylvania Statutes (PA. Stat.), Title 73, beginning with Section (Sec.) 201-1.) The intent of the legislature was to protect consumers from unfair and deceptive trade practices and acts in trade and commerce. The Supreme Court ruled that leasing of residential property falls within the class of business activity that is regulated under this act. (*Commonwealth v. Monumental Properties, Inc.,* 459 Pa. 450, 329 A.2d 812 (1974).)

The court held that use of form leases, without application to the specific facts of a case, did not violate the Consumer Protection Act. Therefore, form leases, in and of themselves, are perfectly valid. The critical issue from a landlord's perspective is that the user of form leases must assure that they are clearly written so as to be fully understandable by the average person (tenant). However, the court found that violations of the law could potentially be found in two specific practices challenged by the Commonwealth. These were:

1. the intentional use of archaic and technical language in form leases to create a likelihood of confusion and misunderstanding on the part of the tenant (329 A.2d at 829-30), and

2. the failure of form leases to notify tenants of the rights under Pennsylvania statutes that could be waived by signing form leases. (329 A.2d at 829.)

Upon a proper factual showing of these practices, a landlord could be subject to penalties for violation of the statute. Thus, observance of the Plain Language Consumer Contract Act, 73 P.S. 2001, should speak to both the unclear language and the failure to notify tenants of attempts at waivers of rights.

The act provides that the tenant may bring a legal complaint seeking money damages for actual monetary losses sustained as a result of a practice found to violate the act. (PA. Stat., Title 73, Sec. 201–9.2.)

SPECIFIC FORM LEASE CLAUSES

The following clauses are currently being included in many form lease agreements in spite of the fact that such clauses may be completely unenforceable under existing law. Landlords often attempt to include the provisions in the hope that the tenant remains uninformed about the unenforceability of such provisions.

Particular case rulings cannot control the use of some of the lease clauses discussed here. In situations that a landlord pursues enforcement of one of those provisions, the tenant must be careful of the facts of the case, and must consider the *adhesion contracts*, discussed on page 67, and requirements for the *waiver of rights*. Section 2 of the Unfair Trade Practices and Consumer Protection Act is applied as well.

LANDLORD'S
RENT
NOTIFICATION
AND DEMAND

Pennsylvania common law rules state that the landlord must establish that a genuine demand for rental payment has been issued to the tenant. Any claim to take back the rented premises or for monetary damages based upon non-payment of rent must first have this proof of demand for rent. (*Elizabethtown Lodge No. 596 v. Ellis*, 391 Pa. 19, 137 A.2d 286 (1958).) To create a case, the landlord must also prove the lease agreement has been terminated for failure to pay rent due *upon demand*. (PA. Stat., Title 68, Sec. 250.501.) The landlord is required to establish that he or she called for the precise rent due on the day upon which it became due.

ADDITIONAL
RENTS

The majority of prewritten form lease agreements contain provisions in which the tenant agrees to relinquish (or give up) any landlord obligation to return portions of rent which may be due to the tenant. This provision is typically found in the section of the form lease agreement entitled "Additional Rents." Observance to the requirement can be chiefly significant to the tenant in a Lease Agreement including a broad termed definition of "additional rents." The tenant has a right to prompt notice of what exact charges the landlord may argue to be "rent." One of the purposes of the requirements of prompt demand for rent is to prevent claims against a tenant for questionable "additional rent" charges claimed by the landlord that appear only after the court battle begins.

NOTE: *The tenant, facing the claim by the landlord, waived request for rent if he or she entered into a prewritten lease form provision contending to give up the right. The tenant should see an attorney.*

HABITABILITY
AND WARRANTY

Various prewritten lease forms waive the obligation of the landlord under the *warranty of habitability*. The warranty of habitability provides that a leased premises will be generally livable and the conditions will not violate health and safety statutes, requirements, or public policies. The landlord, by entering into a lease agreement with the tenant, releases himself or herself from the duty to make repairs. Warranty of habitability provisions in prewritten lease forms may require the *tenant* to carry out all upkeep, or to pay additional rent for all maintenance performed by the landlord.

WAIVER CLAUSE
REGARDING
WARRANTY OF
HABITABILITY

The landlord's responsibilities under the warranty of habitability may not be waived by a lease agreement provision. The commitments cannot be waived as a matter of public policy. (*Fair v. Negley*, 257 Pa. Super. 50, 390 A.2d 240 (1978).)

HOLD
HARMLESS OR
EXCULPATORY
CLAUSES

Countless prewritten lease forms include provisions in which the tenant "agrees" to *hold harmless* the landlord from legal responsibilities in *tort* (negligence) actions. In numerous instances, these clauses have the tenant free the landlord from liability for damages to property or for personal injury caused by the negligence of the landlord. For example, "Tenant agrees to hold harmless the landlord in the even tenant's guest(s) or invitee(s) sustain injury upon sidewalk or entry steps to premises."

Frequently such clauses even provide that the *tenant* will assume liability for injury to the tenant's guests caused by the negligence of the *landlord*. The law sets forth a clear duty on the part of the landlord to remedy known unsafe surroundings in leased property. (*Asper v. Haffley*, 312 Pa. Super. 424, 458 A.2d 1364, 1369-70 (1983).)

ENFORCEABILITY

The Supreme Court in Pennsylvania spoke to the issues of "hold harmless" or "exculpatory clauses" in prewritten lease forms and has ruled as follows:

📖 A clause in a lease agreement that freed the landlord from responsibility for personal injury was held to be in violation of public policy, legally inoperative, and void. The court stated that to rule otherwise would be tantamount to the court lending its power and authority to enforce an agreement to evade compliance with fire prevention statutes. (*Boyd v. Smith*, 372 Pa. 306, 94 A.2d 44, 46 (1953).)

📖 The court ruled that lease agreements that attempt to waive legal rights must be strictly construed against the beneficiaries (landlords) of such agreements and denied enforcement. The opinion went on to note that, because of the adhesionary nature of the form lease, the document could not be construed as representing a "negotiated transaction" reflecting the true intent of the parties. (*Galligan v. Arovitch*, 421 Pa. 301, 304, 219 A.2d 463, 465 (1966).)

📖 The rationale justifying non-enforcement of exculpatory clauses in residential leases may not apply where facts show all parties understood the term made part of a *commercial* lease. (*Princeton Sportswear Cork v. A. & M. Associates*, 510 Pa. 189, 507 A.2d 339, 341 (1986).)

📖 Courts may refuse to enforce exculpatory clauses in contracts between private parties where the clause would encourage offending a public policy of interest to the state or where the parties who executed the document were not in a free bargaining position. In other words, one party merely "adhered" to a form document that he or she was powerless to alter and must reject or accept in total. (*Employers L.A.C. v. Greenville B. Men's A.*, 423 Pa. 288, 291-92, 224 A.2d 620, 622-23 (1966). *Santiago v. Truitt*, 23 D.& C. 3d 313 (1982).)

The Superior Court in *Fair v. Negley* (see page 71), held that as a matter of public policy, the landlord's obligation under the implied warranty of habitability *cannot* be waived by a lease term. One aspect of the landlord's obligations under the warranty must be to *protect* the tenant and guests from dangerous conditions likely to cause physical injury. It would be inconsistent to give effect to a lease clause that allowed the landlord to give up responsibility to protect the tenant from injury caused by the landlord's *own* negligence.

POSSESSION OF THE LEASED PREMISES

As set forth by the common law, the tenant's rights under a lease agreement entails the uninterrupted enjoyment of exclusive possession of the leased property. During the period of tenancy and until the landlord gets the property back after conclusion of the lease term, the tenant can maintain sole and exclusive possession of the property.

The issue of the right to access the leased property by the landlord is often a gray area. Prewritten lease forms that "authorize" the entry by the landlord "at any time" in non-emergencies, causes unreasonable interference with the tenant's rights.

ABANDONMENT

To support a finding that the tenant has abandoned the leased property, the law requires proof of several factors such as the *intention* to abandon, and the *conduct* by which the intention is carried into effect. (*Tumway Corp. v. Soffer*, 461 Fa. 447, 336 A.2d 871,877 (1975).) Intentional abandonment involves more than a temporary absence from the leased property with the intent to reoccupy.

FIXTURES

Prewritten lease forms frequently establish a limit of five or ten days for the tenant's absence from the property. The lease declares such an absence will constitute an abandonment by the tenant. The landlord may then declare a *forfeiture* of the lease and retake the premises.

Deviation from this definition of abandonment may provide a landlord with a basis for an eviction of a tenant. The landlord can assert that he or she is reclaiming possession of leased property in the absence of the tenant, regardless of the tenant's intention to remain in possession.

Recently, legislative proposals have attempted to define explicit factual situations that would establish abandonment. (However, such proposals have not been enacted as of this writing.)

Characteristic prewritten lease form provisions award ownership to all fixtures and improvements installed by the tenant to the landlord or they give the landlord unilateral right to choose to keep them. Narrow application of this type of lease provision would preclude the tenant from claiming that the intent of both parties had been that the tenant would remove the fixtures upon conclusion of the lease agreement.

RETAINING
POSSESSION

Improvements to the leased property affixed, placed, or created by the tenant occasionally cause disputes as to who will remain owner of the fixtures or improvements when the lease agreement ends. Courts will resolve disputes over ownership of fixtures on a case by case basis, by examining the intent of the parties, and utilizing a clear consideration of the practicality of removing the items in dispute.

PENALTY

Penalty provisions in a lease agreement are a type of punishment meant to stop the possibility of a breach of the lease. Settlement or *liquidated damages* are the sum that parties to the lease agreement consent to pay in the occurrence of a breach. Such sum of monies are to be a *good faith* estimation of *actual* damages that might result from a breach. The rationale behind *liquidated damages* is *compensation* as opposed to *retribution*.

NOTE: *Proper lease drafting is critical as the court refuses to enforce penalty provisions, but will enforce liquidated damage clauses.*

Settlement or liquidated damages. Settlement or liquidated damage provisions in residential prewritten lease forms commonly serve to benefit and to protect the landlord. Determination of whether a certain term contained in the lease agreement should be enforced as a liquidated damage provision or whether it is to be disregarded as an unenforceable punishment depends upon the way in which the court views the intent of the parties. Such information will be taken from the lease agreement.

In such analysis, the court must reflect upon the relationship and the sum set forth in the lease agreement to the extent of damages that may be caused by the breach against the ability to measure the damages. Under this study the soundness of a number of ordinary passages in Leases Agreement forms must be reviewed. (*Finkle v. Gulf & Western Mfg. Co.*, 744 F.2d 1015, 1021 (3rd Cir. 1984).)

Late fees. In order to be enforceable as a valid liquidated damages provision, *late fees* must bear a *reasonable relation* to the consequential damages that a landlord incurs in receiving rent late. The loss of use of the rentals for the period of lateness can be valued in monetary terms by reference to interest rates. The landlord's damages would be measured by reference to interest rates if he were to sue to recover the unpaid rentals. (PA. Stat., Title 68, Sec. 250.301.) The landlord should not be able to claim a higher rate of compensation by disguising a penalty charge under the "late fees" label.

In the Commonwealth of Pennsylvania, the legal rate of interest is six per cent per year. The legal rate of interest would equal .5% interest per month for each month of failed or missed rental payment. Assessed late fees of $20 or $30 attached automatically when rent has been missed by a explicit due date create assessments costlier than any "rate" based upon compensation for actual damages.

NOTE: *Such fees are penalties and as such, and should be challenged.*

ACCELERATION OF RENT

Some Commonwealth of Pennsylvania Appellate Court rulings have upheld the validity of rental *acceleration clauses* in lease agreements. (*Pierce v. Hoffsat*, 211 Pa. Super. 380, 236 A.2d 828(1967).) The courts assumed that the clauses represented part of a bargained-for agreement. The tenants did not challenge the voluntariness of the terms nor did they raise the issue of the *adhesion* aspect of the contract.

Parties able to enter into a bargained lease agreement can agree to payment of rent in advance upon the happening of a certain thing, and, as a rule it is the tenant's failure of rental payment. Acceleration provides security to the landlord while the tenant remains in control for the remainder of the period of the lease.

Remedies available to the landlord regarding the acceleration of rent and recovery of control cannot be *cumulative*. This means that because rent acceleration creates a protection for the tenant's future payments while remaining in possession, the landlord cannot at the same time, attempt to take the property away from the tenant or attempt to collect future rent. (*Greco v. Woodlawn Furniture Co.*, 99 Pa. Super. 290, 292 (1930).)

Challenging acceleration of rent provisions. If based on a form contract clause, the acceleration of rent claim may be based on a contract term to which the tenant did not knowingly and voluntarily agree.

   The argument has been made successfully in other jurisdictions that acceleration clauses should not be enforced on the grounds that they are *penalties.* (*Ricker v. Rombough*, 120 Cal. App. 2d Supp. 912, 261 P.2d 328 (1953). *Patton v. Milwaukee Commercial Bank*, 222, Wis. 167,268 N.W. 124 (1936).)

ATTORNEYS'
FEES

In the Commonwealth of Pennsylvania the rule is that, absent an express statutory or contract clause to the contrary, attorneys' fees are plainly discernible and different than costs and are properly borne by the respective parties to the litigation. (*Shapiro v. Magaziner*, 418 Pa. 278, 210 A.2d 890 (1965).)

Statutes in the Commonwealth of Pennsylvania establish procedures for recovery of possession of a leased property that do not contain express clauses that modify the common rule regarding attorneys' fees. (The Pennsylvania Landlord and Tenant Act of 1951, PA. STat., Title 68, Sec. 250.101, and R.C.P. 1051-1058.) Recovery of attorneys' fees in a landlord/tenant case can be awarded to the victorious litigant only in situations in which the parties expressly agreed to a lease provision that changed the Pennsylvania rule. Attorneys' fees claimed must represent the reasonable cost of services that were actually rendered and *cannot* be used as a penalty.

   Attorneys' fees must be reasonable. The court awarding attorneys' fees must evaluate the reasonableness of time spent by the attorney in relation to the particular case. In determining the reasonableness of attorneys' fees, the trial court may examine several factors, including the amount of work performed, the character of the services rendered, and the difficulty of the problems involved. (*In Re Trust Estate of La Rocca*, 431 Pa. 542, 246 A.2d 337, 339 (1968).)

Eviction. In eviction actions based upon non-payment of rent, the issues involved are quite simple. Attorneys who routinely represent landlords appear in local courts to collect *default* judgments or contest an occasional case against an unrepresented tenant. The one-page form complaints can be mass-produced and filled out by an attorney's secretary on the basis of a phone call. The Philadelphia Municipal Court requires the landlord or counsel to certify, by marking or filling in the appropriate box, one or more of the three grounds for eviction:

- the amount of rent claimed;

- termination of term;

- breach of condition; or,

- the absence of Housing Code violations.

The absence of code violations is routinely verified in virtually every municipal court complaint, even though there are a substantial number of cases before that court in which violations are present and recorded by the city. Testimony should be demanded at a district justice or municipal court hearing to establish that a sum claimed for attorney fees represents charges that were reasonable, necessary, and actually accrued. Tenants should not be required to pay excessive fees that bear no relation to the work actually performed. Exorbitant attorney fees are often nothing more than a disguised penalty provision.

Defending claims for attorney fees. There are some suggested challenges to attorney fee claims in which the landlord asserts the fees under a lease agreement clause:

- Attorneys' fees provisions must be stated and clear.

- Claims for attorney fees may be improperly raised on the basis of vague lease terms that do not provide an express notice that they were intended to cover attorneys fees. A universal phrase permitting the landlord to charge the tenant for "costs" or "expenses" associated with a lease violation may not be a sufficient basis for recovery of fees. (*Parkview Court Apts. v. Carr*, 11 D. & C. 3d 791, 795 (1979).)

Ambiguity can also be created where the form lease provides expressly for recovery of attorneys' fees in confession of judgment actions, but does not specifically mention attorneys' fees in other provisions covering recovery of possession through *adversary* or court proceedings.

- The recovery of attorneys' fees in adversary actions cannot be implied from silence particularly where the authors of the lease have shown that they could use express language when they desired to do so.

- The attorney fees provision must be the product of a *bargained-for agreement*.

DEFINING A FORFEITURE OF THE LEASE

Form leases attempt to permit deviations from historic doctrines that have restricted a landlord's right to declare a *forfeiture* of the lease for breach of a lease condition. The declaration of a *forfeiture of the lease upon breach of its conditions* may be a ground for the landlord to get the property back under the Landlord and Tenant Act of 1951, and Pennsylvania Statutes, Title 68, Sections 250.501, and 502. The act does not define the terms *forfeiture* or *condition*. However, the concepts have well-developed meanings from the common law.

📖 Lease conditions are promises by a tenant that he or she will do or refrain from doing some particular thing after taking possession. The tenant's interest can be terminated *(declaration of a forfeiture)* upon breach of a lease condition. (*Williams v. Notopolis*, 259 Pa. 469 (1918).)

A *condition* is to be distinguished from a covenant. A *covenant* is a promise by the tenant, the breach of which does not affect the tenant's possessory interest, but merely gives the landlord the right to sue for money damages. (*Williams v. Notopolis*, 259 Pa. at 475.) The common law distinction between a lease covenant and a lease condition has obvious importance because the landlord cannot seek to evict a tenant for mere breach of a lease *covenant*.

Courts traditionally regarded a lease forfeiture as an extreme remedy and odious to the law. (*Elizabethtown Lodge No. 596 v. Ellis*, 391 Pa. 19, 137; A.2d 286 (1958); *Cimina v. Bronich*, 349 Pa. Super. 399,503 A.2d 427, 429 (1985).) In order to minimize instances of judicial approval of forfeitures, courts developed rules of strict construction *against* lease provisions that could potentially work a forfeiture. Lease promises are construed whenever possible to *avoid* a forfeiture. Ambiguities as to whether a promise in a lease creates a condition or covenant will be resolved in favor of the finding of a covenant. (*Howell v. Sewicklev Twp.*, 352 Pa. 552, 562,43 A.2d 121 (1945).)

Form leases generally seek to get around all common law requirements that a lease condition giving rise to forfeiture be clear and express. Distinctions between conditions and covenants are blurred. Under many form leases, the most trivial infraction of a vague lease promise of the tenant may be construed to work a forfeiture of the leases.

Example: The lease contains a clause where the tenant agrees to act at all times in a manner that the lessor, in its sole "opinion," deems proper and not objectionable. The landlord may declare a forfeiture if the tenant fails to perform any lease covenant or "agreement." These lease "agreements" include "rules and regulations," which the landlord may "at any time," in his or her own judgment, change or introduce to become part of the lease.

Given the extent to which these and similar form lease clauses deviate from established common law principles, their enforcement must be scrutinized closely under the *adhesion contract* and Unfair Trade Practice and Consumer Protection Act analysis outlined in this chapter.

EFFECT OF FORM LEASES

The older form lease contains a provision stating that a custom or practice of the parties contrary to a lease condition shall *never* constitute a waiver of the landlord's right to declare a forfeiture. No matter how long the parties knowingly consented to the practice, and even if the tenant had fixed a breach, this provision would allow the landlord to evict the tenant for conduct that the landlord knowingly let develop. The landlord cannot take advantage of this provision, predominantly in situations where a tenant can show reliance on the landlord's toleration of a pattern of conduct that did not follow the lease. Under these circumstances, courts will refuse to enforce a forfeiture as unconscionable. (*Blue Ridge Metal Mfg. Co. v. Proctor*, 327 Pa. 424, 144 A. 559 (1937).)

HANDLING EVICTIONS 12

The Landlord and Tenant Act of 1951 sets forth mandatory procedures to be followed by a landlord in order to recover possession under the act and evict a tenant. (PA. Stat., Title 68, beginning with Sec. 250.101.) The act provides for some procedural safeguards that benefit the tenant. These include:

- the right to notice prior to starting legal proceedings (PA. Stat., Title 250, Secs. 501, 502);

- the right to appear before a district justice or municipal court judge to present defenses to the landlord's claims (PA. Stat., Title 68, SEc. 250.504); and,

- the right to appeal from the trial court's decision. (PA. Stat., Title 68, Sec. 250.506.)

FORM LEASES   Form leases frequently waive or severely restrict the tenant's procedural rights under the Landlord and Tenant Act. The notice periods may be reduced from ninety to five days, and the rights to appeal judgments or to petition to open judgments are waived. These waivers are *voidable* as adhesionary terms unless the landlord can establish an *intentional and voluntary* waiver of a known legal right. (*Johnson v. Concord Mutual Insurance Co.*, 450 Pa. 614, 300 A.2d 61, 65 (1933).) (See the general discussion of adhesion terms, in Chapter 11.)

Even if representing a valid agreement, waivers of the rights to open judgment and appeal judgments have been very narrowly construed against the landlord. (*Kros v. Bacall Textile Corp.*, 386 Pa. 360, 126 A.2d 421 (1956); *Grady v. Schiffer*, 384 Pa. 302, 121 A.2d 71 (1956).)

LANDLORD EVICTION OF THE TENANT

The landlord can evict the tenant for any one of three reasons:

- the term (usually one month or one year) for which the property was rented is over;

- the tenant is behind in the rent; or,

- the tenant has breached (broken) some clause of the lease agreement.

The landlord needs no reason to evict the tenant if the landlord gives the tenant proper notice that the landlord wants the property back at the end of the term.

PROPER EVICTION PROCEDURE

The Landlord/Tenant Law of 1951 provides the only method by which a landlord may evict the tenant.

Eviction notice. The landlord must give the tenant written notice of the reason for the eviction and the date that the landlord wants the tenant to leave.

NOTE: *The tenant with a written lease agreement should read the lease agreement carefully to see whether or not he or she has given up the right to receive this eviction notice.*

The eviction notice must be personally delivered to the tenant or posted on the dwelling. An eviction notice, sent by mail is probably not enforceable. A written lease agreement may state how many days notice must be given by the landlord before the landlord can evict. If the lease agreement does not state how much notice is required, the general rule is as follows:

- If the term has ended, or it the landlord claims the tenant has breached the lease agreement, the landlord must give the tenant thirty days notice if the lease agreement is for less than one year (this is usually month-to-month), and ninety days notice if the lease agreement is one year or more.

- If the tenant is behind in the rent and has an oral lease agreement with the landlord, the landlord needs to give only fifteen days notice between April 1st and September 1st, but thirty days notice between September 1st and April 1st. If the tenant is not out of the property by the end of the eviction notice, the landlord must follow the procedure through the district justice's office as set forth in the following paragraphs.

Complaint. The form that follows is a *Landlord/Tenant Complaint.* The landlord files the complaint with the appropriate district justice's office, and the landlord receives a yellow copy of the Complaint. The pink copy of the Complaint will be served on the tenant by the constable, who may hand the tenant the Complaint or tape the Complaint to the door of the property. The tenant will also get an orange copy of the same Complaint through the mail. The Complaint says that a hearing will be held at the district justice's office on a particular day and time. The tenant should tell the district justice if the tenant intends to come to the hearing and present his or her side of the case.

The Hearing. At the hearing, both the landlord and the tenant will be put under oath to tell the truth. Either may have a lawyer to present his or her case. The landlord will then take the stand and present his or her case. When the landlord is finished testifying, the tenant can cross-examine the landlord—in other words, ask the landlord any questions the tenant may wish to ask about the case.

When the landlord is finished presenting his or her case, the tenant takes the stand and presents the tenant's side of the case. Again the landlord has the right to question the tenant after the tenant has presented his or her case. Both the landlord and tenant have the right to bring any papers, pictures, or other evidence which is important to prove their case. Either one can also bring any witnesses they may have.

The district justice will decide whether or not the landlord is entitled to a judgment for possession of the property. If the landlord wins his or her case, he or she will get a judgment for possession and the tenant must move out. If the tenant wins, the tenant may stay. The district justice may also decide whether or not either the landlord or the tenant owes the other any money.

If either the landlord or the tenant does not agree with the decision the district justice reaches at the hearing, an appeal can be taken to the local county court house within thirty days after the district justice makes his or her decision. Either the tenant or the landlord will need a lawyer's help in filing this appeal. If either the landlord or the tenant does not attend the hearing he or she will receive notice from the district justice which says what the district justice's decision was and on what date the decision was entered.

Order for Possession. If the landlord wins a *judgment for possession*, the landlord can then enforce the judgment. This means that no sooner than fifteen days after the district justice makes his decision and enters the judgment for possession, the landlord can have the constable give the tenant an order for possession. This order for possession is a notice telling the tenant that unless the tenant is out of the property by a date set on the notice (no sooner than fifteen days after the date the tenant receives the notice) the constable or sheriff can forcibly set the tenant and his or her belongings out of the house or apartment. This is a total of at least thirty days after the judgment for possession was entered.

If the constable has to forcibly evict the tenant, and the tenant has not arranged for a place for his or her furniture and belongings, the sheriff or constable can store the furniture and belongings at a storage company at the tenant's expense. The tenant must pay any storage bill before getting his or her furniture and belongings back. If the tenant does not pay the storage bill or make arrangements regarding the furniture and belongings, they may be sold by the storage company to pay the storage bill.

NOTE: *The landlord may not retain the tenant's furniture or personal belongings or sell them to cover rent owed.*

If the tenant wants to appeal the district justice's decision, the appeal must be filed within thirty days after the judgment for possession has been entered by the district justice. It is then possible to stop the eviction until after the appeal is heard in the Court of Common Pleas. It may be necessary to post a bond unless the court gives permission to waive the bond or to deposit rent instead of a bond. The process of appeal may take several months.

POSSIBLE TENANT DEFENSES TO LANDLORD'S EVICTION

Whenever the landlord sues the tenant, the tenant has the right to defend against the landlord. If the tenant has a good reason to defend against the landlord's suit, the tenant should make every effort to do so, even if the lease agreement says the tenant has no right to defend. If the tenant does not go to the hearing, the landlord wins by default.

The tenant can use the following defenses in the case of an eviction hearing.

- *Failure to Remit Rental Payment.* Rent receipts are the best way to prove that rent has actually been paid. If the tenant used the repair and deduct procedure on page 44, the tenant must bring a copy of the receipt to the hearing. The tenant cannot defend an eviction action based on non-payment of rent because the tenant has withheld rent due to the landlord's failure to make repairs. The tenant can stop an eviction based on non-payment of rent by paying the rent due, plus court costs, at any time before the Constable comes to the door to remove the tenant.

- *Lease Agreement Breach.* If landlord has brought a complaint against the tenant and proved that the tenant has breached the lease agreement, the tenant's only defense is to prove at the hearing that the tenant did not breach (break) the lease agreement.

    Example: If the lease agreement says "no pets" and the tenant brings a dog into the house or apartment, the landlord can claim that the tenant has broken or breached the lease agreement. The tenant may be able to prove that the dog the landlord saw does not belong to the tenant, but perhaps belongs to a neighbor.

    Both the tenant and the landlord should take their lease agreement, any other written papers, and any witnesses to the hearing to help establish their case.

- *End of Term.* At this time in the state of Pennsylvania, there is no defense if the landlord claims that the term of the lease agreement has ended. The landlord must give the tenant proper notice. The landlord's actions should not be in retaliation for any steps the tenant may have taken in the past to enforce the tenant's rights, such as reporting Housing Code violations.

- *Eviction Retaliation.* If the tenant believes he or she is being evicted in retaliation for reporting Housing Code violations or exercising other legal rights, such as joining the tenant's organization, the tenant may want to see a lawyer. Although the general state law in Pennsylvania does not prohibit the landlord from evicting in retaliation, some local laws may prohibit it. The law in many other states has changed so state law may change here, too.

IMPROPER METHODS OF EVICTION

The landlord may inform the tenant that he or she must move immediately or threaten to have the sheriff to throw out the tenant, change the locks, shut off the tenant's electricity, or some other form of self-help eviction.

The landlord cannot legally do anything to evict the tenant other than to follow the procedures through the district justice's office set out above. If the landlord tries any of these other methods, the tenant can seek legal help immediately. When consulting with an attorney, the tenant must show to the attorney the lease agreement, rent receipts, notices, complaints, and/or any other documents.

MOBILE HOME PARKS EVICTION

Residents of mobile home parks in Pennsylvania have special legal rights under a law called the *Mobile Home Park Rights Act*. Under this law, "residents of mobile home parks" are people who are buying or who already own their mobile home and who rent space in a mobile home park containing at least three mobile homes. The law does not cover people who are renting a mobile home. These people have rights under the *Landlord and Tenant Act*.

If the resident owns the mobile home and rents lot space, the resident of a mobile home park can be evicted only for the following reasons:

- nonpayment of lot rent;

- two or more violations of park rules within a six-month period; or,

- the park is closed or the park land is changed to a different use.

To evict a resident for nonpayment of rent, the park owner must notify the resident by certified mail that an eviction case may be started in court unless the resident pays the unpaid rent within twenty days of getting the notice (Thirty days if the notice is given from September 1 to March 31.)

To evict the resident for breaking park rules or for breaking part of the lease agreement, the park owner must first notify the resident by certified mail of the violation. The owner can bring an eviction case in court only if the resident breaks park rules or breaks the lease agreement again within six months.

The park owner must get a court order to evict the tenant. Even if the park owner gets a court order, the tenant still has thirty days to appeal it to a higher court if the tenant has a good reason (defense). The park owner cannot legally evict the tenant in any other manner such as shutting off utilities or padlocking the door. The tenant cannot be evicted based upon exercise of their rights under the *Mobile Home Park Rights Act* or any other legal right.

TENANTS MUST FOLLOW PARK RULES

However, rules must be fair and reasonable and the landlord/owner must:

- give a written copy of the rules;

- post the rules in a place in the park where all residents can read them; and,

- apply the rules equally to all residents.

RESTRICTIONS ON PARK OWNERS

Park owners may not:

- require the tenant to buy undertrailer-skirting, awnings, or other mobile home equipment from one particular supplier. The owner may require a certain type of material and say how this equipment is to be installed;

- prevent the tenant from selling the mobile home. The owner may reserve the right to approve the buyer as a resident of the park. However, the owner cannot unreasonably withhold approval;

- charge any fees for moving the mobile home in or out of the park;

- charge more than the actual cost to install or remove the mobile home;

- charge a fee if the tenant have visitors, unless the visitors stay overnight so often that they can be considered to be living with the tenant; or,

- charge any rent, fees, or service charges that the tenant was not told about in writing at the beginning of the lease agreement. However, the owner can increase rent and service charges by giving written notice to the resident and posting notice of the increase thirty days in advance, or in advance of the end of the lease agreement term, whichever comes later.

SPECIAL RULES FOR FEDERALLY SUBSIDIZED HOUSING

13

This section will provide a brief discussion of the way in which a landlord or tenant's involvement in a federally backed financially subsidized housing program can affect the traditional "landlord/tenant" association. This section primarily summarizes a representative, federally subsidized housing program (known in the Commonwealth of Pennsylvania as Section 8 Existing Housing). After this review, you will find a description of the five authorities that control this financially backed housing policy. The following information will make clear to you the manner in which such procedures affect the landlord/tenant relationship. The five bases of authority are:

1. federal statute;

2. federal regulations;

3. federal administrative agency handbook;

4. local administrative agency administrative plan; and,

5. housing assistance payments contract.

Each of the five sources of legal authority speaks to different portions of the subsidized housing program. By and large, the federal statute provides the purpose and wide-ranging structure of the housing program. Federal regulations illustrate the workings of the program. The federal administrative handbook clarifies the lawmaking agencies that oversee the programs and the way in which the laws relating to the program are to be put into practice.

The administrative strategy depicts the method by which the local administrative bureau has chosen to implement the program necessities. The housing assistance payments contract identifies the connection between the agency paying the housing subsidies and the landlord receiving the payments.

NOTE: *An attorney who represents a private landlord should be attentive to each of these sources of authority before structuring a client's involvement in a subsidized housing program.*

The Subsidized Housing Program (Section 8 Housing Program) of the United States Housing Act of 1937, the United States Code, Title 42, Section 1437f made the subsidized housing program law and established it in Title II of the Housing and Community Development Act of 1974, P.L. 93-383. Originally, the United States Department of Housing and Urban Development (HUD) offered subsidies to a Public Housing Agency (PHA), under an annual contributions contract to administer the Section 8 Existing Housing Program. The PHA provides the HUD rental subsidies to landlords on behalf of qualified tenants in order to facilitate such tenants to rent existing houses or apartments in their neighborhoods.

The procedures of the landlord/tenant features of the Section 8 Existing Housing Program begin when a family applies to PHA for a Certificate of Family Participation. (CFR, Title 24, Sections 982.202 & 203.) If the family is found by the PHA to be qualified to partake of the program and is selected for involvement, it is issued a Voucher of Family Participation. (CFR, Title 24, Section 982.302.) The family then takes its voucher and approaches private landlords to seek their willingness to take part in the program.

The family must locate a unit that:

- meets HUD's quality standards;

- has a rent within HUD'S Fair Market Rent (FMR); and,

- has a landlord willing to participate in the program.

Once the suitable place has been located, the family requests that the PHA approve the lease agreement.

The lease agreement between the family and the private landlord must include a standard lease agreement addendum; must not contain certain prohibited provisions; and, must state the amount of the contract rent that the family must pay to the landlord. (CFR, Title 24, Sec. 982.308.) The landlord and the PHA then execute a Housing Assistance Payments (HAP) contract that requires the PHA to pay the landlord the difference between the family's contribution to the landlord and the contract rent. (CFR, Title 24, Sections 982.311 & .451.)

FEDERAL STATUTES AND REGULATIONS

The function of this public assistance is to aid lower-income families in obtaining a respectable place to reside and to prompt economically mixed housing. The federal statute empowers the secretary of HUD to "enter into annual contribution contracts with public housing agencies pursuant to which such agencies may enter into contracts to make assistance payments to landlords of existing dwelling units. (USC, Title 42, Section 1437f(b)(1).)

Payment of rent. The contract for assistance entered into between the PHA and the landlord creates the maximum monthly rent that includes utilities and all maintenance costs that the landlord is to receive. Such contract establishes the amount of the monthly assistance payment which the landlord is to receive from the PHA and that amount of the rent which the family is required to pay.

Housing assistance payment contracts provisions. The tenant selection is usually at the discretion of the landlord and subject to provisions of annual contributions contract between HUD and the PHA. The PHA may set preferences for admission to the program.

LEASE AGREEMENT

A lease agreement between the tenant and the landlord shall be for at least one year or the term of the contract, whichever is shorter, and shall contain other conditions specified by HUD. (USC, Title 42, Sec. 1437 (d)(1)(B)(i).)

In the course of the period of the lease agreement the landlord shall not terminate the tenancy except for substantial or repeated violations of the provisions and conditions of the lease agreement, or for violation of federal, state, or local laws, or for other good cause.

A lease agreement *can* be terminated for certain types of criminal activity during the term of the lease agreement. (USC, Title 42, Section 1437f(d)(1)(B)(ii).) Termination of the lease agreement however, must be preceded by a written termination notice specifying the grounds for that action.

Maintenance and replacement shall be in accordance with the standard practice for the building concerned as established by landlord and agreed to by PHA.

Rental payments. The total amount of rent a landlord can charge for a unit is covered by the Section 8 Program and is the *contract rent.* For certificates, the amount of the contract rent must be in compliance with both *fair market rent* limitations as determined by the HUD, and rent reasonableness limitations as determined by the PHA. (CFR, Title 24, Sec. 982.305(a)(4) & (5).)

Payment of contract rent. That portion of the contract rent payable by the family is the *tenant rent.* (CFR, Title 24, Section 982.451.) The housing subsidies for vouchers are set at a fixed amount, the *payment standard.* A voucher tenant must pay the difference between the contract rent and the payment standard.

Standards for housing quality. Housing used in the existing housing program must meet the Performance Requirements and Acceptability Criteria. (CFR, Title 24, Sec. 982.401.)

Items covered. Items described in these regulations include sanitary facilities, food preparation and refuse disposal, space and security, thermal environment, illumination and electricity, structure and material, interior air quality, water supply, lead base paint, access, site, neighborhood, sanitary conditions and smoke detectors. (CFR, Title 24, Sec. 982.401(a)(2)(i)(A)-(M)).)

Security deposits. The maximum amount of such deposits, the circumstances in which they may be retained or must be returned, and responsibility to pay interest on such deposits are described in the Code of Federal Regualtions, Title 24, Section 982.313. Such provisions are coordinated with state law.

Lease agreement. The terms of the lease agreement must be approved by the PHA. (CFR, Title 24, Sec. 982.308(b).) Every lease agreement must include all provisions required by HUD.

Prohibited provisions. No lease agreement may contain the following provisions:

- judgment for damages;
- waiver of legal notice by tenant prior to actions for eviction or money judgment;
- waiver of legal proceeding;
- waiver of jury trial;
- waiver of right to appeal judicial error in legal proceedings; or,
- tenant chargeable with cost of legal actions regardless of outcome. (CFR, Title 24, Sec. 982.308(d).)

Condition of the unit. Before a lease agreement and contract approval, the PHA must determine the unit meets the Housing Quality Standards. The lease agreement must specify which utilities are supplied by the landlord and which are to be supplied by the tenant. (CFR, Title 24, Sec. 982.308(e).)

Safeguarding, maintenance, and inspection. Safeguarding, maintenance and inspection of the Section 8 unit is required by the landlord in accordance with the Housing Quality Standards. (CFR, Title 24, Sec. 982.404(a).) Tenants are responsible for maintenance caused by the tenant family and can be terminated from the Section 8 existing program if they fail to remedy such violations of the Housing Quality Standards. Housing Authorities are required to conduct inspections at least annually and as needed in order to insure that the unit meets the Housing Quality Standards. Tenants may complain to the Housing Authority in order to initiate an inspection.

Evictions. During the term of the tenancy, landlords cannot terminate a tenancy, except for specific reasons:

- serious or repeated violation of lease agreement terms;

- violations of applicable federal, state or local laws; or,

- justified basis or good cause. (CFR, Title 24, Sec. 982.310(a).)

The landlord must give a written eviction notice to the tenant family and the housing authority. The notice must explain the grounds for termination of tenancy.

The landlord must give ninety days advance notice to HUD, the housing authority and the tenant family where the termination is for a business or economic good cause or where the HAP contract expires due to insufficient funding. landlords may only evict a tenant by initiating a court action.

GOVERNMENT HANDBOOKS

Governmental agencies which fund or administer subsidized housing programs frequently issue "Handbooks" to guide the implementation of such programs. The U.S. Department of Housing and Development issues a handbook, *Classification Numbers and Indexes*, which lists all of the current handbooks for their various programs.

The Public Housing Agency Administrative Practices Handbook is for the Section 8 Existing Housing Program. This handbook provides guidance to PHA's in the administration of the Section 8 existing housing assistance payment program and provides guidance to HUD Field Offices in program monitoring. Portions of the handbook that use the verbs "shall" and "must" are requirements that are binding. The verbs, "should" and "may" are used to indicate advice.

Housing Assistance Payments Contract (HAP)

The Housing Assistance Payments Contract (HAP) is a written agreement between a PHA and a landlord for the purpose of providing housing assistance payments to the landlord on behalf of an eligible family. (CFR, Title 24, Sec. 982.451).)

The Housing Assistance Payments Contract is a document that compels the landlord to follow the requirements of the Section 8 existing program in return for receiving the HAP payments. The contract includes terms controlling the following matters:

- term of contract (CFR, Title 24, Sec. 982.451 (a)(2));

- amount of contract rent, family portion of rent, HAP portion or rent (CFR, Title 24, Sec. 982.451(b));

- maintenance, operation, inspection (CFR, Title 24, Secs. 982.452 and .453));

- termination of the contract (CFR, Title 24, Sec. 982.454 and .455)); and,

- nondiscrimination in housing. (CFR, Title 24, Sec. 982.457).)

PUBLIC HOUSING EVICTION

Unlike a private landlord, the Housing Authority can only evict the tenant:

- if the tenant is responsible for creating or continuing a threat to the health and safety of other tenants or Housing Authority employees, or

- for "good cause."

What amounts to "good cause" in justifying an eviction depends on the facts of the particular case, but certainly non-payment of rent could be considered "good cause." There can be no eviction based on the end of the term, as there is in a private landlord/tenant relationship.

Before an eviction, the Housing Authority must give the tenant fourteen days written notice if the eviction is for non-payment of rent and thirty days notice for all other reasons. In the notice, the Housing Authority must also state that the tenant has an opportunity to file a *grievance*. This grievance is a written complaint filed by the tenant with the project manager, disagreeing with the Housing Authority's reasons for the proposed eviction.

Once a grievance is filed, the Housing Authority must attempt to settle the matter informally, and then hold a hearing if this informal settlement proves impossible. After the gievance procedure is completed, the Housing Authority must then file a *complaint* with the district justice to complete the eviction process.

The correct procedures for the grievance, and all of the rules and regulations of the project or lease agreement housing, should be posted in the manager's office. It is a good idea for tenants to know these regulations and to refer to them when necessary.

DENIAL OR TERMINATION OF ASSISTANCE

Housing authorities may deny or discontinue assistance to tenant families if:

- the family fails to supply required information;

- the family fails to remedy a housing quality standard violation caused by the family;

- the family fails to allow a housing quality inspection;

- the family commits a serious or repeated violations of the lease agreement;

- the family fails to notify the Housing Authority and the landlord when the family moves or terminates the lease agreement;

- the family fails to notify the Housing Authority when a lease agreement termination notice is received from the landlord;

- the family fails to use the unit as its residence and/or where the family fails to promptly inform the Housing Authority of changes in the family make-up;

- the family fails to notify the Housing Authority about absences from the unit;

- the family has an interest in the unit;

- the family or family member has committed fraud or has otherwise committed a criminal act in connection with the Section 8 program;

- the family or a family member has engaged in drug-related criminal activity; or,

- the family has received other housing assistance while receiving Section 8 assistance.

Housing authorities must provide an informal administrative review process for applicants who are denied assistance. (CFR, Title 24, Sec. 982.554.) Housing authorities must provide an informal administrative hearing process for participating families where, generally, the housing assistance subsidies are being changed, reduced or terminated. (CFR, Title 24, Sec. 982.555(a).) Participating families must be given notice of the change in the subsidy and an opportunity to request an informal hearing. The hearing procedures must be specified in the Housing Authority's administrative plan and must include:

- the right to examine all Housing Authority documents in advance of the hearing;

- the right to a representative at the family's expense; and,

- the right to present evidence and question witnesses.

The hearing officer may not be the person who made or reviewed the decision in question. The reasons for the decision must be issued in a written statement. The decision must be based upon the *preponderance of the evidence* (mere showing of evidence or proof). (CFR, Title 24, Section 982.555(e)(6).)

OTHER SUBSIDIZED HOUSING PROGRAMS

There are a few more Section 8 project-based programs which include:

- New Construction (CFR, Title 24, Part 880);

- Substantial Rehabilitation (CFR, Title 24, Part 881);

- Assistance Payments to State Housing Agencies (CFR, Title 24, Part 883);

- New Construction Set-Asides for Rural Housing Projects (CFR Title 24, Part 884); and,

- Elderly or Handicapped Housing. (CFR, Title 24, Parts 885 and 886.)

The project-based programs are substantially similar to the certificate program with the exception that the subsidy remains with the apartment. If a tenant moves out or is evicted, the tenant will lose the subsidy and the subsidy will then go to the next tenant who moves into the unit. The tenant's share of the rent is generally set at 30% of the tenant's income. (CFR, Title 24, Sec. 880.604.)

The requirements for a lease agreement termination are the same as those found in the certificate program, except that there can be no termination of the lease agreement for expiration of the term for Section 8 project-based lease agreement. The requirements for provisions that must be contained in lease agreement or that may not be contained in lease agreement are identical to the certificate program. The HUD handbook governing the project-based program is *Occupancy Requirements of Subsidized Multifamily Housing Programs, 4350.3.*

DISCRIMINATION LAWS

The Federal Fair Housing Laws of 1968 and 1988 or Title VIII state that it is the policy of the United States to provide, within constitutional limitations, for fair housing throughout the nation. Title VIII protects against the following acts if they are based on race, color, religion, sex, national origin, handicap/disability, and family status.

The following are red-flag areas that reflect breaches of the Federal Fair Housing Laws of 1968 and 1988:

- refusal to sell or rent to, deal or negotiate with, or give truthful information to any person;

- discrimination in the terms, conditions, privileges, provisions of service or facilities in sale or rental or dwelling or property;

- denial of a loan or creation of different terms or conditions for home loans by commercial lenders;

- discriminate, by advertising that housing is available only to persons of a certain race, color, religion, sex, or national origin;

- "block-busting" for profit such as persuading owners to sell or rent housing by telling them that minority groups are moving into the neighborhood; and,

- denial to anyone of the use or participation in, any real estate services, such as brokers' organizations, multiple listing services, or other facilities related to the selling or rent of housing.

GLOSSARY

A

abandonment. When a tenant leaves a rental unit without notice.

acceleration. When all of the future rent becomes due—now.

affidavit of service. Document filed with the court that swears documents were given to a specific person.

appeal. Request to have a judge's decision reviewed by a higher court.

application. Document a prospective tenant completes that gives information about him or her.

asbestos. A material that used to be commonly used in the construction materials of buildings, now known to cause lung damage.

assignee. The person to whom the original tenant assigns all of his or her rights in the rental property.

assignment of a lease. When a tenant gives over all of his rights and most of his responsibilities to another person who "steps into his shoes" and essentially takes his or her place as the tenant.

assignor. The original tenant who assigns his or her rights to another person.

B

bankruptcy. A court order that distributes the debtor's property among creditors and eliminates all outstanding debts.

bargained-for agreement. A mutual agreement or contract between two parties that is voluntary and involves the exchange of consideration (money, goods, services, or a promise for a promise).

breach. Breaking a law, or not doing what one is supposed to do under a contract of lease agreement.

C

cancel. To make a lease void.

case law. Decisions by court that form law.

certificate of occupancy. Document issued by local housing department certifying that a piece of property is fit to be rented as a residence to tenants.

common areas. Areas in an apartment building that are shared by all the tenants, such as the lobby and stairways.

complaint. The legal written notice that begins a civil lawsuit. It gives the person who is charged with doing wrong (the defendant) all the important facts that will be part of the case against him or her.

confession of judgment. The landlord may ask the tenant to sign a lease agreement with a confession of judgment clause. If the tenant signs a lease agreement with this clause, the tenant agrees to let the landlord get a court order against the tenant without giving the tenant notice and a chance for a hearing to present the tenant's side of the story. The court order could say that the tenant owes the landlord money, or that the tenant must move out of the house or apartment. Confession of judgment clauses may also be found in other kinds of contracts, such as retail sales contracts and loan contracts. This procedure may not be enforceable in the courts. If the tenant receives a notice that a judgment has been entered against the tenant, see an attorney immediately.

contracts of adhesion (or adhesion contract). A contract (often a signed form) so imbalanced in favor of one party over the other that there is a strong implication it was not freely bargained. Example: a rich landlord dealing with a poor tenant who has no choice and must accept all terms of a lease, no matter how restrictive or burdensome, since the tenant cannot afford to move.

counterclaim. If one person (the plaintiff) brings a suit against another (the defendant), and the persons being sued (the defendant) has some claim or charge to make against the first (the plaintiff), that charge or claim against the person bringing the suit is called a counterclaim.

credit report. A list of a person's debts that indicates their status and rates the how well the person pays his or her debts.

cure. To fix something, such as a lease violation.

D

damages. Financial loss that a person can sue for in court.

default. Failing to appear in court.

defendent. The person being sued.

defense. A legal response to a court proceeding, an explanation for something.

deregulation. When a rent regulated unit becomes unregulated and the amount of the rent is no longer controlled by law.

demand for rent. A notice served to a tenant requesting payment of late rent or eviction proceedings will be begun.

deposit. Money paid to hold an available rental unit, can also refer to security deposit.

Division of Housing and Community Renewal (DHCR). State agency that govern rent regulated property.

discovery. A period of time during a court case when the parties must share certain requested information with each other.

discrimination. Illegally treating people differently based on personal factors such as race, color, religion, etc.

dishonored check. Check that has insufficient funds or from a closed account.

distraint. The name for the procedure when the landlord takes the tenant's furniture or other belongings and holds them as payment for rent the landlord claims the tenant owes.

This procedure has been held unconstitutional and no landlord should do it. The only procedure to collect back rent is to obtain a judgment and execute on it.

due date. The date rent is due from the tenant to the landlord, determined by the lease or type of rental agreement.

duplex. Rental property with two units.

E

ejectment. Legal remedy that can sometimes be used to remove a person from wrongfully occupying a rental unit or real estate.

escrow account. An account that holds money for a special purpose. In a case of Rent Withholding escrow accounts, the Bureau of Codes Enforcement of City Hall holds the rent money that the tenant pays until certain conditions, such as making the necessary repairs, are met.

evict. To force the tenant to move out of a house or apartment.

execution. The legal way to enforce a judgment. If it is a *judgment for possession*, the sheriff or constable, after giving warning, may forcibly remove the tenant, the tenant's family, and the tenant's furniture and belongings, putting the furniture in storage at the tenant's expense. If it is a *judgment for money*, the plaintiff (person bringing the lawsuit) may, thirty days after the judgment is issued, file the judgment with the county court house. The plaintiff then files a paer called *writ of execution*, which is a paper that asks the sheriff to schedule a sheriff's sale of the tenant's belongings. The sheriff can sell any goods that are not exempt (see *exemption*) and use the money to pay the plaintiff the amount of the judgment plus costs.

exemption. Those belongings of a debtor that are free from *execution*. Pennsylvania law says that no one can take all of another persons' belongings away from him or her by *execution* on a judgment for money arising out of contract. The defendant, or debtor, can keep $300.00 worth of his or her belongings plus his or her personal clothing, a sewing machine, and personal papers. The defendant, or debtor, can decide which belongings he or she will claim which total $300.00. A husband and wife are entitled to $300.00 each, or a total of $600.00.

F

foreclosure. Action by a bank to take possession of real property when payments have not made on a mortgage.

free hold. Any interest in real property which is a life estate or of uncertain or undetermined duration (having no stated end), as distinguished from a leasehold which may have declining value toward the end of a long-term lease (such as the 99-year variety).

H

harassment. A person commits a summary offense when, with intent to harass, annoy or alarm another person, he or she strikes, shoves, kicks or otherwise subjects him to physical contact, or attempts or threatens to do the same; follows a person in or about a public place or places; or, engages in a course of conduct or repeatedly commits acts which alarm or seriously annoy such other person and which serve no legitimate purpose.

holding over. When a tenant remains in a rental property after he or she was legally required to leave.

holdover proceedings. The process a landlord must follow to evict a tenant who has breached the lease.

U.S. Department of Housing and Urban Development (HUD). A federal government agency that works to prevent housing discrimination and provide affordable housing for low-income communities.

I

illegality. When a lease is created for an illegal purpose it cannot be enforced.

implied of habitability. The tenant's obligation to pay rent and the landlord's obligation to maintain habitable (safe, sanitary, and fit) premises depend upon each other. If the landlord violates his obligation to keep the premises in a reasonably fit condition, this may relieve the tenant from his obligation to pay part or all of his rent until the landlord makes all necessary repairs.

impossibility. When circumstances make it impossible for a tenant to move into a rental unit.

improvements. Alterations to a rental unit.

inspection. Visually checking a rental unit.

interest. A percentage that is added to money that remains in a bank account.

inquest. A trial.

J

judgment. Decision by a court.

judgment for money. A ruling of the court, or a court order, that one person in a suit owes the other person a certain amount of money. In landlord/tenant cases. these judgments are most often for back rent, damages. or return of a security deposit.

judgment for possession. The ruling of a court, or a court order, that a person in a suit is entitled to possession of certain property, i.e., to have the right to be in the property. In landlord/tenant suits, either the landlord or the tenant may be awarded the judgment of possession.

jurisdiction. A court's right to hear a specific case.

L

landlord. Property owner who allows the property to be rented.

landlord's right of election. Provides that whatever choice the landlord makes, termination or renewal, becomes binding on him as well. If he elects to hold the tenant to another term, he cannot later change his mind and evict; conversely, if he starts eviction proceedings, it is too late to decide to bind the tenant to a new lease.

lead. A chemical that was formerly used in paint and is now known to be hazardous.

lease agreement. The agreement or contract between landlord and tenant for the possession of the house or apartment being rented. Every landlord and tenant has a lease agreement. The lease agreement can be oral (spoken) or in writing.

leasehold. The real estate that is the subject of a lease (a written rental agreement for an extended period of time). The term is commonly used to describe improvements on real property when the improvements are built on land owned by one party that is leased for a long term (such as 99 years) to the owner of the building.

liability. Legal responsibility.

lien. An entry in county records that will hold a certain amount of money to pay a creditor when the real property it is entered against is sold.

loft. Rental unit created out of a commercial space and occupied by tenants before they were approved as housing.

M

maintenance. Work done to keep a rental property in good condition.

manager. Person hired by a landlord to manage the property and deal with tenants.

manufactured home. A trailer or mobile home.

maximum base rent. The rent that may be charged for a rent regulated unit, it is determined by a formula.

mobile home. A manufactured home that is placed in a mobile home park, where land is rented to place it on.

mobile home owner's bill of rights. State law for mobile home owners found at RPL, Section 233.

modification. A change to the original terms or condition of something.

N

natural wear and tear (normal wear and tear). Even with reasonable and ordinary use, most things will wear out and lose value. This loss of value is called natural wear and tear or normal wear and tear.

non-free hold. Having no interest in real property.

nonpayment. Failure of the tenant to pay rent when it is due.

nonpayment proceedings. The process a landlord must follow to evict a tenant who has failed to pay rent.

notary. A licensed individual who can certify signatures.

notice of appeal. Document filed by the person who loses a court case, asking that a higher court review the decision.

notice of default. A form the landlord gives the tenant stating that the tenant has breached the lease and explains how the tenant can fix the problem.

notice of petition. Form given to defendant, telling him or her when a court proceeding will be heard.

notice of termination. A form served by the landlord on the tenant which gives the tenant a number of days until the lease will be terminated.

O

option to purchase. A tenant's right to purchase the property if he or she chooses (different from right of first refusal).

option to renew. The tenant's right to extend the lease if he or she chooses.

P

petition. Legal form explaining a plaintiff's case.

plaintiff. The person bringing the lawsuit. The person who is suing the defendant.

prepaid rent. Rent that is paid before it is due.

premises. A rental unit.

R

recision. Cancellation of a lease.

renewal. Entering into another lease after the current one has expired.

rent. Money owed by a tenant for the ability to live in the landlord's property.

rent controlled. Buildings with three or more units converted to residential use prior to 1947 and have been continuously occupied by the same tenant or his or her successor since 1971.

rent regulated. Property that is governed by laws that limit the amount of rent and other specifics about the property, includes rent control and rent stabilized units..

rent stabilized. Some properties that were built before 1974 with six or more units.

rental agreement. An agreement that a tenant will rent property from a landlord.

rental unit. Apartment or space being rented.

retaliatory conduct. Actions taken by a landlord to "get back at" a tenant, a form of revenge.

right of first refusal. Tenant's right to be offered the opportunity to purchase the property first before any other potential buyer. If tenant chooses not to purchase, the owner can offer the property to others.

S

satisfaction of judgment. A document filed with the court that indicates a judgment has been paid in full.

security deposit. Money given to the landlord by the tenant to cover any damage the tenant may do to the property during the rental period.
seisin - Possession of a freehold estate in land. Historically, availability of certain remedies for a landowner depended on being able to show seisin. In modern times it is unnecessary to distinguish between seisin and possession, the latter being the basis of most remedies available to a landowner.

seisin. Possession of a freehold estate in land. Historically, availability of certain remedies for a landowner depended on being able to show seisin. In modern times, it is unnecessary to distinguish between seisin and possession, the latter being the basis of most remedies available to a landowner.

self-help. Actions taken by a landlord to remove a tenant without assistance from the court or other authorized personnel.

self-help eviction. Obtaining removal of tenant relief or enforcing one's rights as a landlord without resorting to legal action, such as repossessing a rental unit when payments have not been made or turning off electricity while tenant is still residing in the unit.

self-service storage space. Storage space rented to tenants .

service. legal term for giving someone papers pertaining to a court matter.

single room occupancy (SRO). A single room with a kitchen or bathroom but not both that is rented to a tenant.

statute. A law.

stay. Court order that stops an eviction.

stipulation. An agreement that settles a case.

strict liability. When someone is held legally responsible for something whether or not he or she actually caused it.

sublease. When a tenant rents the unit to someone else for a portion of the lease period.

sublessee. Person who rents the unit from the original tenant.

sublessor. Name for the original tenant when he or she subleases the property out.

sublet, sublease agreement. If the tenant rents the house or apartment to another tenant, the contract or agreement between the first tenant and the second tenant is called a sublease agreement. The first tenant still has responsibility under the original lease agreement unless the landlord agrees to accept the second tenant as a substitute for the first. If the landord does not agree, the first tenant is still responsible to the landlord for any unpaid rent or any damages to the property. Of course, the first tenant can then sue the second tenant to recover the back rent or damages.

summary proceeding. A court proceeding that is shorter than a full blown proceeding.

super (or superintendent). Employee of the landlord who is the tenants' main contact for repairs, rent, etc.

surrender. Giving up possession of rental property.

T

ten day notice to quit. Form given to person occupying unit by landlord giving him or her 10 days to leave the unit or be evicted.

tenancy. The right to occupy real property permanently, for a time that may terminate upon a certain event, for a specific term, for a series of periods until cancelled (such as month-to-month), or at will (which may be terminated at any time). Some tenancy is for occupancy only as in a landlord/tenant situation, or a tenancy may also be based on ownership of title to the property.

tenancy at sufferance. Exists only in one limited situation; where a tenant holds over at the end of a valid lease. This "tenancy" is extremely insubstantial and will end as soon as the landlord exercises his option to either evict or hold the tenant to another term.

tenancy at will. A tenancy that has no stated duration and which may be terminated at any time, by either party.

tenant. Person who rents property from the owner.

term. The period of time that the tenant is entitled to be in the house or apartment under the lease agreement. If there is an oral lease agreement, the term is usually one month, and called month-to-month or year-to-year with the rent being paid in installments each month.

termination. Ending a lease or rental agreement.

U

unavailability. When a rental unit is not available to be lived in at the beginning of the lease, this gives the tenant the right to cancel the lease.

unconscionable. So outrageous it will not be enforced by a court.

V

verification. Form attached to court papers that has the person filing it verify that everything contained in the papers is true.

violation. A condition or act that is in opposition to a term in the lease.

W

waiver. When a party gives up some kind of right; can occur knowingly or unknowingly (such as when a landlord accepts rent after a violation, the landlord waives the right to terminate the rental).

warrant of eviction. Document issued by a court ordering a person to be removed from a rental unit.

warranty of habitability. Requirements about the condition of rental property.

window guards. Bars placed on windows to prevent falls.

witness. Person who formally sees a document being signed.

Appendix A

Pennsylvania Statutes

GENERAL ETHICAL RESPONSIBILITIES

Section (sec.) 35.281. Putting contracts, commitments and agreements in writing.

(a) All contracts, commitments and agreements between a broker, or a licensee employed by the broker, and a principal or a consumer who is required to pay a fee, commission or other valuable consideration shall be in writing and contain the information specified in sec. 35.331 (relating to written agreements generally).

(b) The following are exceptions to subsection (a):

(1) Open listing agreements or nonexclusive buyer agency agreements may be oral if the seller/buyer or landlord/tenant is provided with a written memorandum stating the terms of the agreement.

(2) Transaction licensees or subagents cooperating with listing brokers are not required to obtain a written agreement from the seller/landlord.

(3) Transaction licensees or subagents who provide services to the buyer/tenant but are paid by the seller/landlord or listing broker shall provide, and have signed, a written disclosure statement describing the nature of the services to be performed and containing the information required by section 608 of the act (63 P. S. sec. 455.608).

(c) A licensee may perform services before an agreement is signed, but the licensee is not entitled to recover a fee, commission or other valuable consideration in the absence of a signed agreement.

Authority

The provisions of this sec. 35.281 issued under the Real Estate Licensing and Registration Act (63 P. S. secs. 455.101—455.902); amended under sections 404, 602, 606—606.6 and 608—608.3 of the Real Estate Licensing Registration Act (63 P. S. secs. 455.404, 455.602, 455.606—455.606f and 455.608—455.608c).

Source

The provisions of this sec. 35.281 adopted February 24, 1989, effective February 25, 1989, 19 Pa.B. 781; amended November 17, 2000, effective November 18, 2000, 30 Pa.B. 5954; amended March 29, 2002, effective March 30, 2002, 32 Pa.B. 1644. Immediately preceding text appears at serial page (271735).

Cross References

This section cited in 49 Pa. Code sec. 35.286 (relating to retention and production of records).

[Code of Federal Regulations]   CFR

[Title 24, Volume 4]

[Revised as of April 1, 2001]

From the U.S. Government Printing Office via GPO Access

[CITE: 24CFR982.202]

[Page 569-570]

TITLE 24--HOUSING AND URBAN DEVELOPMENT

CHAPTER IX--OFFICE OF ASSISTANT SECRETARY FOR PUBLIC AND INDIAN HOUSING,

DEPARTMENT OF HOUSING AND URBAN DEVELOPMENT

PART 982--SECTION 8 TENANT BASED ASSISTANCE: HOUSING CHOICE VOUCHER PROGRAM--Table of Contents

Subpart E--Admission to Tenant-Based Program

Sec. 982.202 How applicants are selected: General requirements.

(a) Waiting list admissions and special admissions. The PHA may admit an applicant for participation in the program either:

(1) As a special admission (see Sec. 982.203).

(2) As a waiting list admission (see Sec. 982.204 through

Sec. 982.210).

(b) Prohibited admission criteria--(1) Where family lives. Admission to the program may not be based on where the family lives before admission to the program. However, the PHA may target assistance for families who live in public housing or other federally assisted housing, or may adopt a residency preference (see Sec. 982.207).

(2) Where family will live. Admission to the program may not be based on where the family will live with assistance under the program.

(3) Family characteristics. The PHA preference system may provide a preference for admission of families with certain characteristics from the PHA waiting list. However, admission to the program may not be based on:

(i) Discrimination because members of the family are unwed parents, recipients of public assistance, or children born out of wedlock;

(ii) Discrimination because a family includes children (familial status discrimination);

(iii) Discrimination because of age, race, color, religion, sex, or national origin;

(iv) Discrimination because of disability; or

(v) Whether a family decides to participate in a family self-sufficiency program.

[[Page 570]]

(c) Applicant status. An applicant does not have any right or entitlement to be listed on the PHA waiting list, to any particular position on the waiting list, or to admis-

sion to the programs. The preceding sentence does not affect or prejudice any right, independent of this rule, to bring a judicial action challenging an PHA violation of a constitutional or statutory requirement.

(d) Admission policy. The PHA must admit applicants for participation in accordance with HUD regulations and other requirements, and with PHA policies stated in the PHA administrative plan and the PHA plan. The PHA admission policy must state the system of admission preferences that the PHA uses to select applicants from the waiting list, including any residency preference or other local preference.

[59 FR 36682, July 18, 1994, as amended at 60 FR 34717, July 3, 1995; 61

FR 9048, Mar. 6, 1996; 61 FR 27163, May 30, 1996; 64 FR 26643, May 14,

1999; 65 FR 16821, Mar. 30, 2000]

[Code of Federal Regulations]

[Title 24, Volume 4]

[Revised as of April 1, 2001]

From the U.S. Government Printing Office via GPO Access

[CITE: 24CFR982.452]

[Page 592]

TITLE 24--HOUSING AND URBAN DEVELOPMENT

CHAPTER IX--OFFICE OF ASSISTANT SECRETARY FOR PUBLIC AND INDIAN HOUSING,

DEPARTMENT OF HOUSING AND URBAN DEVELOPMENT

PART 982--SECTION 8 TENANT BASED ASSISTANCE: HOUSING CHOICE VOUCHER PROGRAM--Table of Contents

Subpart J--Housing Assistance Payments Contract and Owner Responsibility

Sec. 982.452 Owner responsibilities.

(a) The owner is responsible for performing all of the owner's obligations under the HAP contract and the lease.

(b) The owner is responsible for:

(1) Performing all management and rental functions for the assisted unit, including selecting a voucher-holder to lease the unit, and deciding if the family is suitable for tenancy of the unit.

(2) Maintaining the unit in accordance with HQS, including performance of ordinary and extraordinary mainte-

nance. For provisions on family maintenance responsibilities, see Sec. 982.404(a)(4).

(3) Complying with equal opportunity requirements.

(4) Preparing and furnishing to the PHA information required under the HAP contract.

(5) Collecting from the family:

(i) Any security deposit.

(ii) The tenant contribution (the part of rent to owner not covered by the housing assistance payment).

(iii) Any charges for unit damage by the family.

(6) Enforcing tenant obligations under the lease.

(7) Paying for utilities and services (unless paid by the family under the lease).

(c) For provisions on modifications to a dwelling unit occupied or to be occupied by a disabled person, see 24 CFR 100.203.

(Approved by the Office of Management and Budget under control number

2577-0169)

[60 FR 34695, July 3, 1995, as amended at 60 FR 45661, Sept. 1, 1995; 63

FR 23861, Apr. 30, 1998; 64 FR 26647, May 14, 1999]

Primary Statute Addressing Landlord Tenant Issues:

Pa. Stat. Ann. tit. 68, secs. 250.101-.510-B

Unconsolidated Pennsylvania Statutes

REAL AND PERSONAL PROPERTY (TITLE 68)

LANDLORD AND TENANT ACT OF 1951

Article I. Preliminary Provisions

[Distraint for unpaid rent has been declared unconstitutional by several courts, including in the cases of Allegheny Clarklift, Inc. v. Woodline Industries of Pennsylvania, Inc., 356 Pa. Superior Ct. 269, 514 A.2d 606 (1986), and Ragin v. Schwarts, 393 F. Supp. 152 (1975).]

LANDLORD AND TENANT ACT OF 1951

sec. 250.201. Leases for not more than three years.

Real property, including any personal property thereon, may be leased for a term of not more than three years by a landlord or his agent to a tenant or his agent, by oral or written contract or agreement.

sec. 250.203. Assignment, grant and surrender of leases to be in writing; exception.

No lease of any real property made or created for a term of more than three years shall be assigned, granted or surrendered except in writing signed by the party assigning, granting or surrendering the same or his agent, unless such assigning, granting or surrendering shall result from operation of law.

sec. 250.205. Participation in Tenants Association.

No individual unit lease on residential property shall be terminated or nonrenewed on the basis of the participation of any tenant or member of the tenant's family in a tenants' organization or association.

sec. 250.206. Statement of Escrowed Funds.

Whenever an agency or department certifies that a dwelling is uninhabitable and a tenant elects to pay rent into an escrow account established under the act of January 24, 1966 (1965 P.L. 1534, No. 536; 35 P.S. sec. 1700-1), referred to as the City Rent Withholding Act, it shall be the duty of the certifying agency or department to submit a monthly statement of escrowed funds to the landlord affected by first class mail.

LANDLORD AND TENANT ACT OF 1951

sec. 250.202. Leases for more than three years.

Real property, including any personal property thereon, may be leased for a term of more than three years by a landlord to a tenant or by their respective agents lawfully authorized in writing. Any such lease must be in writing and signed by the parties making or creating the same, otherwise it shall have the force and effect of a lease at will only and shall not be given any greater force or effect either in law or equity, notwithstanding any consideration therefor, unless the tenancy has continued for more than one year and the landlord and tenant have recognized its rightful existence by claiming and admitting liability for the rent, in which case the tenancy shall become one from year to year.

sec. 250.203. Assignment, grant and surrender of leases to be in writing; exception.

No lease of any real property made or created for a term of more than three years shall be assigned, granted or surrendered except in writing signed by the party assigning, granting or surrendering the same or his agent, unless such assigning, granting or surrendering shall result from operation of law.

sec. 250.205. Participation in Tenants Association.

No individual unit lease on residential property shall be terminated or nonrenewed on the basis of the participation of any tenant or member of the tenant's family in a tenants' organization or association.

sec. 250.206. Statement of Escrowed Funds.

Whenever an agency or department certifies that a dwelling is uninhabitable and a tenant elects to pay rent into an escrow account established under the act of January 24, 1966 (1965 P.L. 1534, No. 536; 35 P.S. sec. 1700-1), referred to as the City Rent Withholding Act, it shall be the duty of the certifying agency or department to submit a monthly statement of escrowed funds to the landlord affected by first class mail.

Appendix B
Landlord Checklist

The following is a sample list of things to inspect both when a tenant moves in and out of the premises. This double-inspection is done to determine what needs repair upon move-in, and whether something was damaged during the tenancy.

CHECKLIST FOR LANDLORD/OWNER/MANAGER
DURING MOVE-IN AND MOVE-OUT INSPECTIONS

	In Good Condition	No.	Needs Repair	No.
LIVING ROOM				
Doors	_____	_____	_____	_____
Windows	_____	_____	_____	_____
Walls	_____	_____	_____	_____
Floors	_____	_____	_____	_____
Ceiling/Roof	_____	_____	_____	_____
Rug/Carpet	_____	_____	_____	_____
Electrical Installations	_____	_____	_____	_____
Furniture	_____	_____	_____	_____
BEDROOMS				
Doors	_____	_____	_____	_____
Windows	_____	_____	_____	_____
Walls	_____	_____	_____	_____
Floors	_____	_____	_____	_____
Ceiling/Roof	_____	_____	_____	_____
Rugs/Carpet	_____	_____	_____	_____
Electrical Installations	_____	_____	_____	_____
Furniture	_____	_____	_____	_____
Closets	_____	_____	_____	_____
KITCHEN				
Doors	_____	_____	_____	_____
Windows	_____	_____	_____	_____
Walls	_____	_____	_____	_____
Ceiling/Roof	_____	_____	_____	_____

Floor   _____   _____   _____   _____

Electrical Installations   _____   _____   _____   _____

Cabinets   _____   _____   _____   _____

Range/Oven   _____   _____   _____   _____

Refrigerator   _____   _____   _____   _____

Sink   _____   _____   _____   _____

Plumbing/Pipes   _____   _____   _____   _____

Other Appliances   _____   _____   _____   _____

Rodents/Cockroaches   _____   _____   _____   _____

BATHROOM

Doors   _____   _____   _____   _____

Windows   _____   _____   _____   _____

Walls   _____   _____   _____   _____

Floor   _____   _____   _____   _____

Roof/Ceiling   _____   _____   _____   _____

Bathtub/Shower   _____   _____   _____   _____

Electrical Installations   _____   _____   _____   _____

Electric Outlets   _____   _____   _____   _____

Sink   _____   _____   _____   _____

Toilet   _____   _____   _____   _____

Plumbing/Pipes   _____   _____   _____   _____

OTHER

Halls   _____   _____   _____   _____

Stairs/Steps   _____   _____   _____   _____

Windows   _____   _____   _____   _____

Window Curtains   _____   _____   _____   _____

Screen   _____   _____   _____   _____

Windows/Doors	_____	_____	_____	_____
Storm Windows	_____	_____	_____	_____
Paint	_____	_____	_____	_____
Heating Unit	_____	_____	_____	_____
Locks	_____	_____	_____	_____
Outside Balcony/Railing	_____	_____	_____	_____
Safety Locks/Chains	_____	_____	_____	_____
Window Locks	_____	_____	_____	_____
Banister	_____	_____	_____	_____
Porch	_____	_____	_____	_____

Appendix C
Landlord's Obligations to the Tenant

Since landlord/tenant law varies by state, the key is to be knowledgeable about your rights and duties in Pennsylvania—before you draft your lease agreement or rental agreement. Understanding the provisions that can be placed in a lease agreement is the best guarantee to safeguard against future difficulties.

Lease agreement requirements are uniform and common to all locales. Following you will find a sampling of rights applicable in Pennsylvania:

- Residential rental units should be habitable and in compliance with housing and health codes, meaning they should be structurally safe, sanitary, weatherproofed, and include adequate water, electricity, and heat.

- The landlord should make necessary repairs and perform maintenance tasks in a timely fashion, or include a provision in the lease agreement stating that tenants can order repairs and deduct the cost from rent.

- The landlord must give prior notice (typically twenty-four hours) before entering tenant premises and can normally only do so to make repairs or in case of an emergency.

- Illegal provisions in a rental agreement (provisions counter to state law) are usually not enforceable in court.

- If the landlord has violated important terms related to health, safety, or necessary repairs, the tenant might have a legal right to break the lease agreement.

- If the tenant breaks a long-term lease agreement, landlords are required to search for a new tenant as soon as possible rather than charging the tenant for the full duration of the lease agreement.

- Damage or security deposits are not deductible for "normal wear and tear."

- Landlords are legally prohibited from evicting tenants as retaliation for action the tenant takes related to a perceived landlord violation.

- The landlord cannot legally change the locks, shut off (or cause to have shut off) utilities, or evict without notice. Eviction requires a court order.

- It is illegal for a lease agreement to stipulate that the tenant is responsible for the landlord's attorney fees in case of a court dispute.

APPENDIX D
LANDLORD/TENANT
RESOURCES

HARRISBURG FAIR HOUSING COUNCIL
1228 Bailey Street
Harrisburg, PA 17103
717-238-9540

CITY OF HARRISBURG DEPARTMENT OF COMMUNITY & ECONOMIC DEVELOPMENT
Bureau of Codes Enforcement
4th Floor, Room 406
Martin Luther King Jr.,
City Government Center
Harrisburg, PA 17101

To report problems with the Landlord (by welfare recipients) contact the:
DEPARTMENT OF PUBLIC ASSISTANCE
2432 N. 7th Street (Dauphin County office)
Harrisburg, PA 17110
717-787-4550
717-787-2324

PENNSYLVANIA DEPARTMENT OF CONSUMER PROTECTION
Strawberry Square
14th Floor
Harrisburg, PA 17101
717-787-7109

PENNSYLVANIA HUMAN RELATIONS COMMISSION
Regional Office
2971-E N. 7th St.
Harrisburg, PA 17110
717-787-9780
717-787-9784

HARRISBURG HUMAN RELATIONS COMMISSION
City Public Safety Building
123 Walnut Street
2nd Floor, Suite 235
Harrisburg, PA 17101
717-255-3037

HELP/Harrisburg Emergency Lifeline Program
234 South St.
Harrisburg, PA 17101
238-2851

APPENDIX E
SUBSIDIZED HOUSING

Further information about Landlord-Tenant Law is available at the Harrisburg Fair Housing Council, 1228 Bailey Street Harrisburg, Pa. 17102, phone: 717-238-9540

The Harrisburg Housing Authority provides public housing in projects and scattered leased houses in various sections of the capital city for families, elderly, and handicapped who have low incomes. Questions and applications should be made at:

Morrison Towers
351 Chestnut Street
Harrisburg, PA
717-232-6781

The Dauphin County Housing Authority also provides low-income housing outside the city of Harrisburg. Questions and applications should be made at:

Latsha Towers
501 Mohn Street
Steelton, PA
717-939-9301

Other forms of rental assistance are available for persons with slightly higher incomes in government subsidized rental housing.

Other subsidized housing complexes that provide rental assistance:

DAUPHIN COUNTY

Presbyterian Apartments
(Age 50 and Older, Handicapped)
Harrisburg
717-233-5114

Linden Terrace
(Elderly and Handicapped)
Harrisburg
717-232-4454

Pheasant Hill Estates
(Elderly)
Harrisburg
717-657-3135

B'Nai Brith Apartments
(Elderly)
Harrisburg
717-232-7516

Hummelstown Manor
Hummelstown
717-566-8782

Middletown Interfaith Apts.
(Elderly)
Middletown
717-944-7634

Edison Village
(Family, Elderly and Handicapped)
Harrisburg
717-232-0564

East Bridge Apartments
(Family and Elderly)
Harrisburg
717-561-0364

Maclay Street Apartments
(Family, Elderly and Handicapped)
Harrisburg
717-238-1553

Rutherford Park
(Elderly and Family)
Harrisburg
717-561-0615

Harrisburg Park Apartments
(Family)
Harrisburg
717-236-5184

Cumberland Court Apartments
(Family, Elderly and Handicapped)
Harrisburg
717-232-0571

Parkside Apartments
(Family and Elderly)
Harrisburg
717-232-7438

CUMBERLAND COUNTY

One West Penn
(Elderly and Handicapped)
Carlisle
717-249-7797

Meadowbrook Apartments
(Elderly and Handicapped)
Mechanicsburg
717-697-9517

Susquehanna View Apts.
(Elderly)
Camp Hill
717-763-1184

Bethany Towers
(Elderly and Disabled)
Mechanicsburg
717-766-7698

Orchard Apartments
(Family and Handicapped)
Camp Hill
717-763-0937

APPENDIX F
FORMS

Tenant Rental Application

Each occupant over 18 years old is a co-applicant and considered a tenant and must submit a separate application.

Date when filled out: _____

ABOUT YOU:

Full name (exactly as on driver's license or govt. ID card): _____

Tenant address as shown on Tenant driver's license or govt. ID card:

Street Address: _____

City/State/Zip: _____

Driver's license # and state or govt. photo ID card #: _____

Birthday: _____ Height: _____ Sex: Male ❑ Female ❑ Soc. Sec. #: _____

Tenant current home address (If apartment, give name):

Street Address: _____

City/State/Zip: _____

Phone: (_____)_____ Current monthly rent: $ _____

Current owner or manager's name: Current Owner or Manager's Phone: (_____)_____

Date moved in: _____

Why are you leaving current residence?_____

Tenant previous home address (If apartment, give name):

Street Address: _____

City/State/Zip: _____

Phone: (_____)_____ Monthly rent: $ _____

Previous owner or manager's name: Previous Owner or Manager's Phone: (_____)_____

Date moved in: _____

TENANT WORK:

Present employer: _____

Tenant employer's address: _____

Street Address: _____

City/State/Zip: _____

Tenant position: Phone: (_____)_____

Tenant gross monthly income: $_____ Date you began this job: _____

Supervisor's name: Supervisor's phone number: (_____)_____

Previous employer: _____

Previous employer's address:

Street Address: _____

City/State/Zip: _____

Tenant position: _____ Tenant gross monthly income: $ _____

Date you began this job: _____ Date you ended this job: _____

Supervisor's name: Supervisor's phone number: (_____)_____

TENANT CREDIT HISTORY:

Tenant bank's name, city, state: _____

List major credit cards: _____

Tenant other non-work income you want considered. Please explain: _____

_____

Have you ever owned a home? ❐ Yes ❐ No

Past credit problems you want to explain. (Use separate page if you need more space):

_____

_____

TENANT RENTAL/CRIMINAL HISTORY:

Check the box for any question that that Tenant answer is yes. Please explain all questions answered yes (use separate page if you need more space).

Have you ever:

❏ been evicted or asked to move out?

❏ broken a rental agreement?

❏ declared bankruptcy?

❏ been found liable for failure to pay rent or for property damage?

❏ been convicted of a felony or sex-related crime?

CO-APPLICANT:

Full name (exactly as on driver's license or govt. ID card): _____

Tenant address as shown on Tenant driver's license or govt. ID card:

Street Address: _____

City/State/Zip: _____

Driver's license # and state or govt. photo ID card #: _____

Former last names: _____

Birthday: _____ Height: Sex: Male ❏ Female ❏ Soc. Sec. #: _____

Present employer: _____

Employer's address:

Street Address: _____

City/State/Zip: _____

Position: Phone: (_____)_____

Gross monthly income: $_____ Date began this job:_____

Supervisor's name: Supervisor's phone number: (_____)_____

OTHER OCCUPANTS:

List the names of all persons under 18 and other adults who will occupy the unit without signing the lease. _____

Continue on separate page if more than three.

Full name (exactly as on driver's license or govt. ID card): _____

Address (if different from Tenants):

Street Address: _____

City/State/Zip: _____

Driver's license # and state or govt. photo ID card #: _____

Birthday: Sex: Male ❑ Female ❑ Soc. Sec. #: _____

Full name (exactly as on driver's license or govt. ID card): _____

Address (if different from Tenants):

Street Address: _____

City/State/Zip: _____

Driver's license # and state or govt. photo ID card #: _____

Birthday: Sex: Male ❑ Female ❑ Soc. Sec. #: _____

Full name (exactly as on driver's license or govt. ID card): _____

Address (if different from Tenants):

Street Address: _____

City/State/Zip: _____

Driver's license # and state or govt. photo ID card #: _____

Birthday: Sex: Male ❑ Female ❑ Soc. Sec. #: _____

TENANT VEHICLES:

List all vehicles to be parked by you or any occupants (including cars, trucks, motorcycles, trailers, etc.). _____

Continue on separate page if more than one.

Make, model and color of vehicle: _____ Year: _____

State and License Number: _____

OTHER INFORMATION:

Will you or any occupant have a pet animal? ❐ yes ❐ no If yes, you must complete an Pet Addendum with this application. All animals must be approved by the Landlord or Agent in advance.

Do you or does any occupant smoke? ❐ yes ❐ no

How were you referred?

❐ Internet

❐ stopped by

❐ rental publication (name: _____)

❐ rental agency/locator service (agency name: _____
  Agent's name: _____)

❐ Friend (name:)

❐ Newspaper (name _____)

❐ Other (name)

EMERGENCY:

Emergency contact person over 18, who will not be living with you:

Name: _____

Street Address: _____

City/State/Zip: _____

Phone: (____)_____ Relationship: _____

If you die or are seriously ill, missing, or in a jail or penitentiary according to an affidavit of (check one or more): ❐ the above person, ❐ Tenant spouse, or ❐ Tenant parent or child, we may allow such person(s) to enter Tenant dwelling to remove all contents, as well as Tenant property in the mailbox, storerooms, and common areas. If no box is checked, any of the above is authorized at our discretion. If you are seriously ill or injured, you authorize us to send for an ambulance at Tenant expense. We are not legally obligated to do so.

If you become seriously ill or injured, what doctor may we notify? (We are not responsible for providing medical information to or calling doctors or emergency personnel.)

Doctor's name: _____

Phone: (_____)_____

Street Address: _____

City/State/Zip: _____

Important medical information about you in an emergency:

AUTHORIZATION:

I or we authorize the Landlord, agent and/or the apartment management to verify the above information, including, but not limited to, Tenant credit history, by all available means. Owner is not required to re-verify or investigate preliminary findings.

Applicant's signature _____

Co-Applicant's signature _____

INSPECTION REPORT
THE FOLLOWING INSPECTION SHOULD BE COMPLETED PROMPTLY FOLLOWING INITIAL OCCUPANCY OR UPON DELIVERY OF POSSESSION

The parties acknowledge that the attached inspection was made on _____, and that the conditions of the premises and the inventory of furnishings and appliances is shown above. The parties further agree that a copy of this Joint Inspection was provided to Lessee/Tenant.

Landlord Name:_____   Tenant

Name:_____

_____ [Lessors]   _____

[Lessee]

PREMISES: [State Address of Property]

DATE OF POSSESSION: [Move in Date]   Clean   ND - No Damage   ENB - Exception Noted Below   C - Checkout

LIVING ROOM	CL	ND	ENB	C	BATHROOM - 1	CL	ND	ENB	C
Walls & Baseboard	( )	( )	( )	( )	Walls & Baseboard Sink	( )	( )	( )	( )
Hardwood Floor	( )	( )	( )	( )	Counter	( )	( )	( )	( )
Drapes, Rods & Hooks	( )	( )	( )	( )	Cabinets/Mirror	( )	( )	( )	( )
Door & Lock	( )	( )	( )	( )	Toilet	( )	( )	( )	( )
Coat Closet	( )	( )	( )	( )	Bath Tub/Shower	( )	( )	( )	( )
					Light Fixture	( )	( )	( )	( )
DINING AREA					Floor	( )	( )	( )	( )
Walls & Baseboard	( )	( )	( )	( )	Tissue Holder/Towel Bars	( )	( )	( )	( )
Hardwood Floor	( )	( )	( )	( )					
Light Fixture	( )	( )	( )	( )	BATHROOM - 2				
Windows & Screens	( )	( )	( )	( )	Walls & Baseboard Sink	( )	( )	( )	( )
					Counter	( )	( )	( )	( )
KITCHEN					Tissue Holder/Towel Bars	( )	( )	( )	( )
Walls & Baseboards	( )	( )	( )	( )	Toilet	( )	( )	( )	( )
Light Fixture	( )	( )	( )	( )	Light Fixture	( )	( )	( )	( )
Stove					Floor	( )	( )	( )	( )
Drip Pans	( )	( )	( )	( )					
Oven	( )	( )	( )	( )	BEDROOM 1 - MASTER				
Broiler Pan	( )	( )	( )	( )	Built-in Recessed Cupboard	( )	( )	( )	( )
Hood, Fan & Light	( )	( )	( )	( )	Walls & Baseboards	( )	( )	( )	( )
Refrigerator	( )	( )	( )	( )	Windows & Screens	( )	( )	( )	( )
Defrosted	( )	( )	( )	( )	Drapes, Rods & Hooks	( )	( )	( )	( )
Ice Trays (2)	( )	( )	( )	( )	Light Fixtures	( )	( )	( )	( )
Hydrator Cover	( )	( )	( )	( )	Carpet	( )	( )	( )	( )
Dishwater	( )	( )	( )	( )	Closet	( )	( )	( )	( )
Cupboards	( )	( )	( )	( )					
Drawers	( )	( )	( )	( )	BEDROOM 2 - (DEN)				
Counter	( )	( )	( )	( )	Walls and Baseboards	( )	( )	( )	( )
Sink	( )	( )	( )	( )	Windows & Screens	( )	( )	( )	( )
Disposal & Stopper	( )	( )	( )	( )	Hardwood Floor	( )	( )	( )	( )
Floor	( )	( )	( )	( )	Drapes, Rods & Hooks	( )	( )	( )	( )
Water Purifier	( )	( )	( )	( )	Light Fixtures	( )	( )	( )	( )
					Closet	( )	( )	( )	( )
HALL									
Walls & Baseboards	( )	( )	( )	( )					
Hardwood Floor	( )	( )	( )	( )	SOLARIUM				
Light Fixture	( )	( )	( )	( )	Walls & Baseboards	( )	( )	( )	( )
Linen Closet	( )	( )	( )	( )	Windows & Screens	( )	( )	( )	( )
					Drapes, Rods & Hooks	( )	( )	( )	( )
LAUNDRY AREA					Light Fixtures	( )	( )	( )	( )
Washer	( )	( )	( )	( )	Marble Floor	( )	( )	( )	( )
Dryer	( )	( )	( )	( )	Hot Tub	( )	( )	( )	( )
Other/Range-top stove	( )	( )	( )	( )	Balcony/Patio	( )	( )	( )	( )
Storage Area	( )	( )	( )	( )					

Exceptions:

FURNITURE INVENTORY (If the furniture is provided by Landlord)

LIVING ROOM	No.	DINING AREA	No.	BEDROOMS	No.
Couch	_____	Table	_____	Beds	_____
Chairs	_____	Chairs	_____	Dressers	_____
Lamps	_____	Hutch	_____	Mirrors	_____
Coffee Table	_____	Bookcases	_____		
End Table	_____				

OTHER	KITCHEN	No.
_____	Stove	_____
_____	Oven	_____
_____	Refrigerator	_____
_____	Dishwasher	_____
_____	Table	_____
_____	Chairs	_____

House-Duplex Lease Agreement

Herein referenced House Duplex Lease Agreement (" House Duplex Lease") is made and effective [Date], by and between [Lessor] and [Tenant].

Lessor desires to lease the Property to Tenant, and Tenant desires to acquire the House Duplex for lease.

THEREFORE, for value received by each of the parties hereto, the receipt and sufficiency of which are hereby respectively acknowledged, and in consideration of the mutual agreements of the parties, it is hereby agreed:

HOUSE DUPLEX LEASE

1.   Lessor agrees to lease the House Duplex as follows:

House Duplex Lease Term: [Term of Lease] Monthly Rent: [Monthly Rent Paid by Tenant]

2.   Tenant shall pay the rent to Lessor not later than the [Rent Due Date] day of each month. Rent payments shall be made to the address for Lessor below or such other address that Lessor may identify to Tenant from time to time. Tenant shall also pay to Lessor any other amount or charge that Lessor is obligated to pay under the Lease that arises or is attributable to Tenant's occupancy such as, but not limited to, charges for garbage, water sewer, utilities, common area expenses, maintenance and trash removal. Such charges shall be paid within ten days of Lessor's statement. Tenant shall be responsible for procuring and paying for any utilities or services not provided by landlord pursuant to the Lease.

3.   In the event there is more than one Tenant party, then the obligations of each such Tenant shall be joint and several.

USE OF LEASED FURNISHINGS AND PERSONAL PROPERTY

-Obligations Under House Duplex Lease Agreement-

Tenant agrees to comply with the terms of the Lease and shall not do or permit to be done anything that would constitute a breach or default of Lessor's regulations. Lessor agrees, provided Tenant is not in breach or default of any obligation in this House Duplex Lease, that Lessor shall not do anything to disturb Tenant's use of the leased Premises.

Hold Harmless Clause

Tenant will indemnify, protect, defend and hold lessor harmless from and against any and all loss, cost, damage and expense arising out of or in any way related to a breach or default of Lessor's regulations.

4. TERM OF LEASE

The term of this House Duplex Lease Agreement shall initiate on [Date], and conclude on the [End Date]. In the event that Lessor is unable to provide the Rental Unit on the initiation date, then Landlord shall provide the Rental Unit as soon as practicable, and Tenant's obligation to pay rent shall halt during such period. Tenant shall not be entitled to any other remedy for any delay by Lessor in providing the Rental Unit.

5. RENTAL PAYMENTS

Tenant agrees to pay, without demand, to Lessor as rent for the Rental Unit the sum of [Monthly Rent] per month in advance on the first day of each calendar month, at [Address for Rental Payments], or at such other place as Lessor may designate. Lessor may impose a late payment charge of [Late Pay Charge] per day for any amount that is more than five (5) days late. Rent will be pro-rated if the term does not start on the first day of the month or for any other partial month of the term.

6. SECURITY DEPOSIT

Upon execution of this Lease, Tenant deposits with Lessor[Security Deposit Amount], as security for the performance by Tenant of the terms of this Lease to be returned to Tenant, [With or Without Interest], following the full and faithful performance by Tenant of this Lease. In the event of damage to the Rental Unit caused by Tenant or Tenant's family, agents or visitors, Lessor may use funds from the deposit to repair, but is not limited to this fund and Tenant remains liable.

7. USE OF PREMISES

Rental Unit shall be used and occupied by Tenant exclusively as a private single-family House Duplex. Neither the Rental Unit nor any part of the Rental Unit or premises shall be used at any time during the term of this Lease for the purpose of carrying on any business, profession, or trade of any kind, or for any purpose other than as a private single-family residence. Tenant shall comply with all the health and sanitary laws, ordinances, rules, and orders of appropriate governmental authorities and homes associations, if any, with respect to the Rental Unit.

Lessor _____

Tenant _____

Date _____

APARTMENT LEASE AGREEMENT

Herein referenced Apartment Lease Agreement (" Apartment Lease") is made and effective [Date], by and between [Lessor] and [Tenant]. Lessor desires to lease the Property to Tenant, and Tenant desires to acquire the apartment for lease.

THEREFORE, for value received by each of the parties hereto, the receipt and sufficiency of which are hereby respectively acknowledged, and in consideration of the mutual agreements of the parties, it is hereby agreed:

APARTMENT LEASE

1.   Lessor agrees to lease the apartment as follows:

Apartment Lease Term: [Term of Lease] Monthly Rent: [Monthly Rent Paid by Tenant]

2.   Tenant shall pay the rent to Lessor not later than the [Rent Due Date] day of each month. Rent payments shall be made to the address for Lessor below or such other address that Lessor may identify to Tenant from time to time. Tenant shall also pay to Lessor any other amount or charge that Lessor is obligated to pay under the Lease that arises or is attributable to Tenant's occupancy such as, but not limited to, charges for garbage, water sewer, utilities, common area expenses, maintenance and trash removal. Such charges shall be paid within ten days of Lessor's statement. Tenant shall be responsible for procuring and paying for any utilities or services not provided by landlord pursuant to the Lease.

3.   In the event there is more than one Tenant party, then the obligations of each such Tenant shall be joint and several.

USE OF LEASED FURNISHINGS AND PERSONAL PROPERTY

Obligations Under Apartment Lease Agreement-

Tenant agrees to comply with the terms of the Lease and shall not do or permit to be done anything that would constitute a breach or default of Lessor's regulations. Lessor agrees, provided Tenant is not in breach or default of any obligation in this Apartment Lease, that Lessor shall not do anything to disturb Tenant's use of the leased Premises.

Hold Harmless Clause

Tenant will indemnify, protect, defend and hold lessor harmless from and against any and all loss, cost, damage and expense arising out of or in any way related to a breach or default of Lessor's regulations.

4. TERM OF LEASE

The term of this Apartment Lease Agreement shall initiate on [Date], and conclude on the [End Date]. In the event that Lessor is unable to provide the Rental Unit on the initiation date, then Landlord shall provide the Rental Unit as soon as practicable, and Tenant's obligation to pay rent shall halt during such period. Tenant shall not be entitled to any other remedy for any delay by Lessor in providing the Rental Unit.

5. RENTAL PAYMENTS

Tenant agrees to pay, without demand, to Lessor as rent for the Rental Unit the sum of [Monthly Rent] per month in advance on the first day of each calendar month, at [Address for Rental Payments], or at such other place as Lessor may designate. Lessor may impose a late payment charge of [Late Pay Charge] per day for any amount that is more than five (5) days late. Rent will be pro-rated if the term does not start on the first day of the month or for any other partial month of the term.

6. SECURITY DEPOSIT

Upon execution of this Lease, Tenant deposits with Lessor[Security Deposit Amount], as security for the performance by Tenant of the terms of this Lease to be returned to Tenant, [With or Without Interest], following the full and faithful performance by Tenant of this Lease. In the event of damage to the Rental Unit caused by Tenant or Tenant's family, agents or visitors, Lessor may use funds from the deposit to repair, but is not limited to this fund and Tenant remains liable.

7. USE OF PREMISES

Rental Unit shall be used and occupied by Tenant exclusively as a private single-family apartment. Neither the Rental Unit nor any part of the Rental Unit or premises shall be used at any time during the term of this Lease for the purpose of carrying on any business, profession, or trade of any kind, or for any purpose other than as a private single-family residence. Tenant shall comply with all the health and sanitary laws, ordinances, rules, and orders of appropriate governmental authorities and homes associations, if any, with respect to the Rental Unit.

Lessor _____

Tenant _____

Date _____

RESIDENTIAL (RENTAL) LEASE AGREEMENT

This Residential Lease Agreement ("Lease") is made and effective this [Date] by and between [Landlord] and [Tenant]. This Residential Lease Agreement creates joint and several liability in the case of multiple Tenants which means each Tenant is responsible for the acts of the others and remain liable wholly for all damages or breaches to the premises or Lease.

1. PREMISES--

Landlord hereby agrees to rent to Tenant and Tenant accepts in its present condition the Rental Unit at following [Rental Unit Address] address (the "Rental Unit").

2. TERM OF LEASE

The term of this Residential Lease Agreement shall initiate on [Date], and conclude on the [End Date]. In the event that Landlord is unable to provide the Rental Unit on the initiation date, then Landlord shall provide the Rental Unit as soon as practicable, and Tenant's obligation to pay rent shall halt during such period. Tenant shall not be entitled to any other remedy for any delay by Landlord in providing the Rental Unit.

3. RENTAL PAYMENTS

Tenant agrees to pay, without demand, to Landlord as rent for the Rental Unit the sum of [Monthly Rent] per month in advance on the first day of each calendar month, at [Address for Rental Payments], or at such other place as Landlord may designate. Landlord may impose a late payment charge of [Late Pay Charge] per day for any amount that is more than five (5) days late. Rent will be pro-rated if the term does not start on the first day of the month or for any other partial month of the term.

4. SECURITY DEPOSIT

Upon execution of this Lease, Tenant deposits with Landlord [Security Deposit Amount], as security for the performance by Tenant of the terms of this Lease to be returned to Tenant, [With or Without Interest], following the full and faithful performance by Tenant of this Lease. In the event of damage to the Rental Unit caused by Tenant or Tenant's family, agents or visitors, Landlord may use funds from the deposit to repair, but is not limited to this fund and Tenant remains liable.

5. USE OF PREMISES

Rental Unit shall be used and occupied by Tenant exclusively as a private single-family residence. Neither the Rental Unit nor any part of the Rental Unit or yard shall be used at any time during the term of this Lease for the purpose of carrying on any business, profession, or trade of any kind, or for any purpose other than as a private single-family residence. Tenant shall comply with all the health and sanitary laws, ordinances, rules, and orders of appropriate governmental authorities and homes associations, if any, with respect to the Rental Unit.

6. NUMBER OF INHABITANTS

Tenant agrees that the Rental Unit shall be occupied by no more than [Total Number of Inhabitants] persons, including no more than [Maximum Number of Children] under the age of eighteen (18) years, without the prior written consent of Landlord.

7. QUIET ENJOYMENT OF PREMISES

Landlord agrees that on paying the rent and performing the obligations contained in this Lease, Landlord will not interfere with Tenant's peaceful use and enjoyment of the Rental Unit.

Lessor _____

Tenant _____

Date _____

LANDLORD'S CONSENT TO ASSIGNMENT

The undersigned party, as owner and lessor of the real property in the Lease Agreement dated [Date] between [Tenant] as tenant ("Assignor") and the undersigned [Landlord], as Landlord, a copy of which is attached hereto ("Lease"), hereby agrees and consents to the assignment of the Lease by Assignor to [Assignee]. The undersigned party does not agree nor consent to any further assignment or subletting of the Leased premises.

The undersigned hereby certifies in respect of the Lease that:

The Assignor is tenant under the Lease and the Lease Agreement as attached hereto is in full force and effect and Assignor is not in default thereof.

In the event that Assignee exercises the option to extend or renew the Lease, or if Assignee agrees to extend or renew the Lease, the undersigned party does hereby release Assignor, from any liability to the undersigned party under the terms and conditions of said Lease Agreement which accrue and become due during the extended term or period.

_____

[Landlord]

This page intentionally left blank

TENANT'S ASSIGNMENT OF LEASE AGREEMENT

This Tenant's Assignment of Lease Agreement ("Agreement") is made and effective [Date] by and between

[Assignor] ("Assignor"), and [Assignee] ("Assignee").

Assignor is the tenant in a Lease Agreement dated [Date] with [Landlord's Name] a copy of which is attached hereto (the "Lease"). Assignor now desires to assign its interest in the Lease to Assignee, which Assignee desires to acquire.

THEREFORE, for value received by each of the parties hereto, the receipt and sufficiency of which are hereby respectively acknowledged, and in consideration of the mutual agreements of the parties, it is agreed:

Assignment—

Assignor has a leasehold interest as tenant or lessee in the Lease. Assignor does hereby grant, bargain, sell, convey, transfer and assign to Assignee all of the leasehold estate as created and evidenced by the Lease, and all of Assignor's interest therein, including all rights, privileges, appurtenances, options to renew, options to purchase, deposits, prepaid rentals, monies and obligations now or hereafter owing from Assignor's landlord.

Assumption by Assignee—

Assignee assumes and agrees to perform all of the duties of tenant or lessee under the Lease, which accrue and become due on and after the date hereof, and Assignee will indemnify, protect, defend and hold Assignor harmless from and against any and all loss, cost, damage and expense arising out of or in any way related to a breach or default of the Lease after the date hereof, and Assignor will indemnify, protect, defend and hold Assignee harmless from and against any and all loss, cost, damage and expense arising out of or in any way related to a breach or default of the Lease on or before the date hereof.

3. Notices—

Any notice given in connection with this Agreement, shall be in writing and shall be given to the appropriate party by personal delivery or by certified mail, postage prepaid, or recognized overnight delivery services.

To Assignor:

[Assignor] _____

[Assignor's Address] _____

To Assignee:

[Assignee] _____

[Assignee's Address] _____

IN WITNESS WHEREOF, the parties hereto have caused this Agreement to be duly executed as of the date first above written.

Signed by:

_____

[Assignor]

_____

[Assignee]

Landlord's Rules and Regulations

[Landlord's Name]

a. Doorways, vestibules, halls, stairways, sidewalks, and comparable areas shall not be blocked; nor shall refuse, furniture, boxes, and/or other items be placed therein by Tenant or its agents, assigns, servants, and/or employees; or utilized for any purpose other than inward-bound and outward-bound travel from the Leased Premises, or for going from one part of the Building to another part of the Building. Soliciting, petitioning, and peddling on the premises are prohibited.

b. Fixtures such as plumbing and the like, and appliances shall be used only for the purposes for which intended, and no unsuitable material shall be placed within same. Tenant assumes liability and responsibility for the upkeep, maintenance, and repair of said fixtures and appliances, including but not limited to sinks, garbage disposals, toilets, hot water heaters, and dishwashers.

c. No posted signs, directories, posters, advertisements, or notices shall be painted or affixed on or to any of the window or doors, or in corridors or other parts of the Building, except as shall be first approved in writing by Landlord. No additional signs shall be posted without Landlord's prior written consent as to location and form, and the cost of preparing and posting such sign shall be borne solely by Tenant. Landlord shall have the right to remove all unapproved signs without notice to Tenant, at the expense of Tenant.

d. Tenants shall not act, or permit anything to be done in or about the Building, or bring or keep anything therein, that will in any way increase the rate of fire or other insurance on the Building, or on premises or otherwise increase the possibility of fire or other loss.

e. Landlord shall have the power to prescribe the weight and position of heavy equipment or objects which may overstress any portion of the floor. All damage done to the Leased Premises or the Building by the improper placing of such heavy items will be repaired at the sole expense of the responsible Tenant.

f. Moving-in or moving-out of Tenant's equipment, furniture, and/or fixtures shall be done only with prior written notice to Landlord, and the Landlord shall be entitled to prescribe the hours of such activity, the elevators which shall be available for such activity and shall, in addition, be entitled to place such other conditions upon Tenant's moving activities as Landlord deems appropriate. Tenant shall bear all risk of loss relating to damage incurred with respect to Tenant's property in moving, and, further, shall indemnify and hold harmless Landlord as to all losses, damages, claims, causes of action, costs, and/or expenses relating or resulting from personal injury or property damage sustained by Landlord or any third party on account of Tenant's moving activities.

g. Corridor or hallway doors, when not in use, shall be kept closed.

h. Deliveries must be made via the service entrance and elevators, designated by Landlord for service, if any, during normal working hours. Landlord's written approval must be obtained for any delivery outside of regular hours.

i. Tenant shall cooperate with Landlord in keeping the Leased premises clean. Landlord may employ a cleaning service for the Leased premises or the Building. Landlord is not responsible for losses caused by any such service.

_____

Dated

[Date]

[Tenant]

[Tenant's Address]

Statement of Repairs

Dear [Tenant]:

This correspondence comes to notify you that repairs must be made as a result of your residency and use (outside of normal wear and tear) of the rental unit.

In accordance with your Lease Agreement and your contractual obligation, you are required to make payments for damages done to the rental unit while same was under your occupancy and control. Thus, the following are repairs which must be made to return the premises to the condition in which it had been (excluding normal wear and tear) at the time of your occupancy.

[List repairs to be made]

Accordingly, your security deposit shall be adjusted to reflect the cost of the aforestated repairs.

Very truly yours,

_____

[Landlord]

This page intentionally left blank

LANDLORD'S NOTICE OF CHANGE OF TERMS
AMENDMENT TO LEASE/RENTAL AGREEMENT

The undersigned party, as Landlord/owner and lessor of the real property in the Lease Agreement dated [Date] between [Landlord] and [Tenant], a copy of which is attached hereto ("Lease"), hereby agrees and consents to the change of Terms/amendment(s) contained in the Lease to be amended as follows:

[State amendments/changes to Original Lease]

The undersigned hereby certifies in respect of the Original Lease that:

The Tenant under the Original Lease/ Lease Agreement as attached hereto is in full force and effect and said Tenant is not in default thereof.

In the event that Tenant exercises the option to extend or renew the Lease, the undersigned parties do hereby adopt and ratify the new terms as hereinabove stated. All other terms as set forth in the Original Lease Agreement are incorporated by reference and made a part hereof, and as such, they remain in full force and effect.

_____

[Landlord]

_____

[Tenant]

Date _____

This page intentionally left blank

SUBLEASE AGREEMENT

Herein referenced Sublease Agreement ("Sublease") is made and effective [Date], by and between [Sublessor] and [Subtenant].

Sublessor is the tenant in a Lease Agreement dated [Master Lease Date] with [Landlord's Name] for a term ending [Lease End Date]. A copy of the Master Lease is attached hereto and incorporated herein by reference. The property leased to Sublessor in the Master Lease is referred to as the Leased Property.

Sublessor now desires to sublease the Leased Property to Subtenant, and Subtenant desires to acquire the sublease.

THEREFORE, for value received by each of the parties hereto, the receipt and sufficiency of which are hereby respectively acknowledged, and in consideration of the mutual agreements of the parties, it is hereby agreed:

SUBLEASE

1.   Sublessor agrees to sublease the Leased Property as follows:

Sublease Term: [Term of Lease] Monthly Sublease Rent: [Monthly Rent Paid by Subtenant]

2.   Subtenant shall pay the rent to Sublessor not later than the [Rent Due Date] day of each month. Rent payments shall be made to the address for Sublessor below or such other address that Sublessor may identify to Subtenant from time to time. Subtenant shall also pay to Sublessor any other amount or charge that Sublessor is obligated to pay under the Master Lease that arises or is attributable to Subtenant's occupancy such as, but not

limited to, charges for garbage, water sewer, utilities, common area expenses, maintenance and trash removal. Such charges shall be paid within ten days of Sublessors statement. Subtenant shall be responsible for procuring and paying for any utilities or services not provided by landlord pursuant to the Master Lease.

3.   In the event there is more than one Subtenant party, then the obligations of each such Subtenant shall be joint and several.

USE OF LEASED FURNISHINGS AND PERSONAL PROPERTY

-Obligations Under Master Lease-

Subtenant agrees to comply with the terms of the Mater Lease and shall not do or permit to be done anything that would constitute a breach or default of Sublessors obligations in the Master Lease. Sublessor agrees to comply with all of Sublessor's obligations in the Master Lease regarding that part of the Leased Property that is not subleased to Subtenant. Sublessor agrees timely to pay rent and other charges due under the Master Lease and, provided Subtenant is not in breach or default of any obligation in this Sublease, shall not do anything to disturb Subtenant's use of the Subleased Premises.

Hold Harmless Clause

Subtenant will indemnify, protect, defend and hold Sublessor harmless from and against any and all loss, cost, damage and expense arising out of or in any way related to a breach or default of Sublessor's obligations in the Master Lease by Subtenant.

LANDLORD'S ANNUAL LETTER OF REGULATIONS AND CONTINUATION OF TENANCY

Dear [Tenant]

Your Lease Agreement term expires on [Date]. Accordingly, you are invited to renew your Lease Agreement for another term of ___ year/months [state desired term].

Rental rates for the term commencing on your renewal date shall be [state Rental Rate].

All other terms and conditions remain in full force and effect. Accordingly, the regulations which apply to your leased premises are as follows.

a. Doorways, vestibules, halls, stairways, sidewalks, and comparable areas shall not be blocked; nor shall refuse, furniture, boxes, and/or other items be placed therein by Tenant or its agents, assigns, servants, and/or employees; or utilized for any purpose other than inward-bound and outward-bound travel from the Leased Premises, or for going from one part of the Building to another part of the Building. Soliciting, petitioning, and peddling on the premises are prohibited.

b. Fixtures such as plumbing and the like, and appliances shall be used only for the purposes for which intended, and no unsuitable material shall be placed within same. Tenant assumes liability and responsibility for the upkeep, maintenance, and repair of said fixtures and appliances, including but not limited to sinks, garbage disposals, toilets, hot water heaters, and dishwashers.

c. No posted signs, directories, posters, advertisements, or notices shall be painted or affixed on or to any of the window or doors, or in corridors or other parts of the Building, except as shall be first approved in writing by Landlord. No additional signs shall be posted without Landlord's prior written consent as to location and form, and the cost of preparing and posting such sign shall be borne solely by Tenant. Landlord shall have the right to remove all unapproved signs without notice to Tenant, at the expense of Tenant.

d. Tenants shall not act, or permit anything to be done in or about the Building, or bring or keep anything therein, that will in any way increase the rate of fire or other insurance on the Building, or on premises or otherwise increase the possibility of fire or other loss.

e. Landlord shall have the power to prescribe the weight and position of heavy equipment or objects which may overstress any portion of the floor. All damage done to the Leased Premises or the

Building by the improper placing of such heavy items will be repaired at the sole expense of the responsible Tenant.

f. Moving-in or moving-out of Tenant's equipment, furniture, and/or fixtures shall be done only with prior written notice to Landlord, and the Landlord shall be entitled to prescribe the hours of such activity, the elevators which shall be available for such activity and shall, in addition, be entitled to place such other conditions upon Tenant's moving activities as Landlord deems appropriate. Tenant shall bear all risk of loss relating to damage incurred with respect to Tenant's property in moving, and, further, shall indemnify and hold harmless Landlord as to all losses, damages, claims, causes of action, costs, and/or expenses relating or resulting from personal injury or property damage sustained by Landlord or any third party on account of Tenant's moving activities.

g. Corridor or hallway doors, when not in use, shall be kept closed.

h. Deliveries must be made via the service entrance and elevators, designated by Landlord for service, if any, during normal working hours. Landlord's written approval must be obtained for any delivery outside of regular hours.

i. Tenant shall cooperate with Landlord in keeping the Leased premises clean. Landlord may employ a cleaning service for the Leased premises or the Building. Landlord is not responsible for losses caused by any such service.

Signed _____

    [Landlord]

Date_____

Notice to Tenant of Security Deposit Holdings

Upon execution of this your Lease Agreement (Lease), Tenant deposits with Landlord [Security Deposit Amount], as security for the performance by Tenant of the terms of this Lease to be returned to Tenant, [With or Without Interest], following the full and faithful performance by Tenant of this Lease. In the event of damage to the Rental Unit caused by Tenant or Tenant's family, agents or visitors, Landlord may use funds from the deposit to repair, but is not limited to this fund and Tenant remains liable.

Tenant funds are held at the following Banking institution _____.

Check one that applies:

___ Tenant shall receive _____% interest on security deposit computed in accordance with the rule of the Commonwealth of Pennsylvania pertaining to holding security deposit funds.

___ Tenant agrees that he/she shall receive no (0%) interest on to security deposit funds held.

_____

[Landlord]

_____

[Tenant]

Date _____

This page intentionally left blank

NOTICE TO QUIT

[Date]

[Tenant]

[Tenant's Address]

Dear [Tenant]:

This correspondence comes to notify you that you are in now default of your contractual obligation to make rental payments as set forth and clearly provided in our Lease Agreement made [Date of Lease] for the property at [Address of Leased Property]. For the reason of this herein stated default, I hereby demand that you quit, vacate, yield, and relinquish the property at once.

This Notice to Quit does not release you from any of your obligations under the Lease Agreement, and it is not a waiver or forfeiture of any right or remedy under the Lease Agreement, at law, in equity, or for any other default.

Very truly yours,

_____

[Landlord]

This page intentionally left blank

LETTER OF TERMINATION OF LEASE AGREEMENT

Dear Tenant:

This Letter serves as a Termination of Lease communication and constitutes an Agreement is made and effective this [Date], by and between [Landlord] and [Tenant].

Landlord and Tenant are parties to that certain [Lease Agreement Title] dated [Lease Date] regarding the property commonly known and numbered [Property Address] (the "Leased Premises").

The parties now desire to provide for the termination of the Lease and the return of the Leased Premises to Landlord, prior to the expiration of the term of the Lease.

In consideration of the mutual promises hereinbelow contained, the parties hereto agree as follows:

Landlord and Tenant are each in compliance with their respective obligations pursuant to the Lease including, without limitation, Tenant's obligation to pay rent, excepting only: [Description of Outstanding Defaults]. The foregoing defaults, if any, shall be cured by the defaulting party on or before the "Termination Date" (set forth below).

The parties agree that the Lease shall terminate on [Date Lease Will Terminate] (the "Termination Date"). On or before the Termination Date, Tenant shall pay Landlord the following amount: [Termination Charge]. Not later than the Termination Date, Tenant shall quit the Leased Premises and shall surrender and return the Leased Premises to Landlord in good condition and repair, reasonable wear and tear excepted. Tenant shall also return to Landlord all keys provided to Tenant by Landlord in connection with the Leased Premises. Tenant also agrees that all of Tenant's personal property shall be removed from the Leased Premises by the Termination Date.

The parties agree that each shall continue to perform the party's individual obligations contained in the Lease including, but not limited to, Tenant's obligation to pay rent, through the Termination Date. If the Termination Date is other than the last day of the month, then the parties agree that the rent attributable to that part of the month through the Termination Date shall be pro-rated, based upon the daily rate.

This Agreement shall be for the benefit of, and shall be binding upon, the parties hereto and their heirs, executors, administrators and assigns.

Excluding obligations, if any, to cure the default set forth in Section 1 above, each party hereby releases Agreements, discharges and waives its right with respect to any claim arising out of or in any way connected with the Lease Agreement, whether known or unknown, through the date of this Agreement.

Signed _____
      Landlord

Date_____

LANDLORD'S NOTICE TERMINATING TENANCY

[Date]

[Tenant]

[Tenant's Address]

Re: Notice of Termination

Dear [Tenant]:

You currently occupy the property at [Address of Leased Property] pursuant to a month-to-month tenancy. This correspondence comes to notify you that your tenancy in and of the property is terminated effective [Termination Date].

Please be certain that you have vacated the property and removed all of your personal items by the stated termination date. Further, please be certain that the property and premises are surrendered clean and in the same condition as when your occupancy commenced. Reasonable wear and tear is allowable. All keys must also be returned by the stated termination date. Further, please be advised that you remain fully responsible for the payment of rent through the termination date. You are not allowed to apply the unresolved amount of Security Deposit toward rental payment.

I thank you for your cooperation in vacating and surrendering the property/premises as stated in this notice.

Very truly yours,

_____

[Landlord]

This page intentionally left blank

[Date]

[Landlord]

[Landlord's Address]

TENANT'S NOTICE OF TERMINATION

Dear [Landlord]:

I am currently the tenant at [Address of Leased the "Premises"] pursuant to a month-to-month tenancy.

This is to notify you that I am hereby terminating my tenancy and I shall vacate the Premises effective [Date of Termination]. Please be advised that the premises will be returned to you on that date. I will also return all keys at the above-stated date. My forwarding address is as follows: [Provide new address]

[Rent and Deposits]

Very truly yours,

_____

[Tenant]

INDEX

SPHINX® PUBLISHING ORDER FORM

BILL TO:		SHIP TO:	
Phone #	Terms	F.O.B. Chicago, IL	Ship Date

Charge my: ☐ VISA ☐ MasterCard ☐ American Express

☐ **Money Order or Personal Check**

Credit Card Number

Expiration Date

Qty	ISBN	Title	Retail	Ext.
		SPHINX PUBLISHING NATIONAL TITLES		
	1-57248-148-X	Cómo Hacer su Propio Testamento	$16.95	
	1-57248-226-5	Cómo Restablecer su propio Crédito y Renegociar sus Deudas	$21.95	
	1-57248-147-1	Cómo Solicitar su Propio Divorcio	$24.95	
	1-57248-238-9	The 529 College Savings Plan	$16.95	
	1-57248-166-8	The Complete Book of Corporate Forms	$24.95	
	1-57248-163-3	Crime Victim's Guide to Justice (2E)	$21.95	
	1-57248-159-5	Essential Guide to Real Estate Contracts	$18.95	
	1-57248-160-9	Essential Guide to Real Estate Leases	$18.95	
	1-57248-139-0	Grandparents' Rights (3E)	$24.95	
	1-57248-188-9	Guía de Inmigración a Estados Unidos (3E)	$24.95	
	1-57248-187-0	Guía de Justicia para Víctimas del Crimen	$21.95	
	1-57248-103-X	Help Your Lawyer Win Your Case (2E)	$14.95	
	1-57248-164-1	How to Buy a Condominium or Townhome (2E)	$19.95	
	1-57248-191-9	How to File Your Own Bankruptcy (5E)	$21.95	
	1-57248-132-3	How to File Your Own Divorce (4E)	$24.95	
	1-57248-083-1	How to Form a Limited Liability Company	$22.95	
	1-57248-231-1	How to Form a Nonprofit Corporation (2E)	$24.95	
	1-57248-133-1	How to Form Your Own Corporation (3E)	$24.95	
	1-57248-224-9	How to Form Your Own Partnership (2E)	$24.95	
	1-57248-232-X	How to Make Your Own Simple Will (3E)	$18.95	
	1-57248-200-1	How to Register Your Own Copyright (4E)	$24.95	
	1-57248-104-8	How to Register Your Own Trademark (3E)	$21.95	
	1-57248-233-8	How to Write Your Own Living Will (3E)	$18.95	
	1-57248-156-0	How to Write Your Own Premarital Agreement (3E)	$24.95	
	1-57248-230-3	Incorporate in Delaware from Any State	$24.95	
	1-57248-158-7	Incorporate in Nevada from Any State	$24.95	
	1-57071-333-2	Jurors' Rights (2E)	$12.95	
	1-57248-223-0	Legal Research Made Easy (3E)	$21.95	
	1-57248-165-X	Living Trusts and Other Ways to Avoid Probate (3E)	$24.95	
	1-57248-186-2	Manual de Beneficios para el Seguro Social	$18.95	
	1-57248-220-6	Mastering the MBE	$16.95	

Qty	ISBN	Title	Retail	Ext.
	1-57248-167-6	Most Valuable Bus. Legal Forms You'll Ever Need (3E)	$21.95	
	1-57248-130-7	Most Valuable Personal Legal Forms You'll Ever Need	$24.95	
	1-57248-098-X	The Nanny and Domestic Help Legal Kit	$22.95	
	1-57248-089-0	Neighbor v. Neighbor (2E)	$16.95	
	1-57248-169-2	The Power of Attorney Handbook (4E)	$19.95	
	1-57248-149-8	Repair Your Own Credit and Deal with Debt	$18.95	
	1-57248-217-6	Sexual Harassment: Your Guide to Legal Action	$18.95	
	1-57248-219-2	The Small Business Owner's Guide to Bankruptcy	$21.95	
	1-57248-168-4	The Social Security Benefits Handbook (3E)	$18.95	
	1-57248-216-8	Social Security Q&A	$12.95	
	1-57248-221-4	Teen Rights	$22.95	
	1-57071-399-5	Unmarried Parents' Rights	$19.95	
	1-57248-161-7	U.S.A. Immigration Guide (4E)	$24.95	
	1-57248-192-7	The Visitation Handbook	$18.95	
	1-57248-225-7	Win Your Unemployment Compensation Claim (2E)	$21.95	
	1-57248-138-2	Winning Your Personal Injury Claim (2E)	$24.95	
	1-57248-162-5	Your Right to Child Custody, Visitation and Support (2E)	$24.95	
	1-57248-157-9	Your Rights When You Owe Too Much	$16.95	
		CALIFORNIA TITLES		
	1-57248-150-1	CA Power of Attorney Handbook (2E)	$18.95	
	1-57248-151-X	How to File for Divorce in CA (3E)	$26.95	
	1-57071-356-1	How to Make a CA Will	$16.95	
	1-57248-145-5	How to Probate and Settle an Estate in California	$26.95	
	1-57248-146-3	How to Start a Business in CA	$18.95	
	1-57248-194-3	How to Win in Small Claims Court in CA (2E)	$18.95	
	1-57248-196-X	The Landlord's Legal Guide in CA	$24.95	
		FLORIDA TITLES		
	1-57071-363-4	Florida Power of Attorney Handbook (2E)	$16.95	
	1-57248-176-5	How to File for Divorce in FL (7E)	$26.95	
	1-57248-177-3	How to Form a Corporation in FL (5E)	$24.95	
	1-57248-203-6	How to Form a Limited Liability Co. in FL (2E)	$24.95	
	1-57071-401-0	How to Form a Partnership in FL	$22.95	

Form Continued on Following Page   **SUBTOTAL**

To order, call Sourcebooks at 1-800-432-7444 or FAX (630) 961-2168 (Bookstores, libraries, wholesalers—please call for discount)
Prices are subject to change without notice.
Find more legal information at: **www.SphinxLegal.com**

SPHINX® PUBLISHING ORDER FORM

Qty	ISBN	Title	Retail	Ext.
	1-57248-113-7	How to Make a FL Will (6E)	$16.95	
	1-57248-088-2	How to Modify Your FL Divorce Judgment (4E)	$24.95	
	1-57248-144-7	How to Probate and Settle an Estate in FL (4E)	$26.95	
	1-57248-081-5	How to Start a Business in FL (5E)	$16.95	
	1-57248-204-4	How to Win in Small Claims Court in FL (7E)	$18.95	
	1-57248-202-8	Land Trusts in Florida (6E)	$29.95	
	1-57248-123-4	Landlords' Rights and Duties in FL (8E)	$21.95	

GEORGIA TITLES

Qty	ISBN	Title	Retail	Ext.
	1-57248-137-4	How to File for Divorce in GA (4E)	$21.95	
	1-57248-180-3	How to Make a GA Will (4E)	$21.95	
	1-57248-140-4	How to Start a Business in Georgia (2E)	$16.95	

ILLINOIS TITLES

Qty	ISBN	Title	Retail	Ext.
	1-57248-206-0	How to File for Divorce in IL (3E)	$24.95	
	1-57248-170-6	How to Make an IL Will (3E)	$16.95	
	1-57248-247-8	How to Start a Business in IL (3E)	$21.95	
	1-57248-252-4	The Landlord's Legal Guide in IL	$24.95	

MASSACHUSETTS TITLES

Qty	ISBN	Title	Retail	Ext.
	1-57248-128-5	How to File for Divorce in MA (3E)	$24.95	
	1-57248-115-3	How to Form a Corporation in MA	$24.95	
	1-57248-108-0	How to Make a MA Will (2E)	$16.95	
	1-57248-106-4	How to Start a Business in MA (2E)	$18.95	
	1-57248-209-5	The Landlord's Legal Guide in MA	$24.95	

MICHIGAN TITLES

Qty	ISBN	Title	Retail	Ext.
	1-57248-215-X	How to File for Divorce in MI (3E)	$24.95	
	1-57248-182-X	How to Make a MI Will (3E)	$16.95	
	1-57248-183-8	How to Start a Business in MI (3E)	$18.95	

MINNESOTA TITLES

Qty	ISBN	Title	Retail	Ext.
	1-57248-142-0	How to File for Divorce in MN	$21.95	
	1-57248-179-X	How to Form a Corporation in MN	$24.95	
	1-57248-178-1	How to Make a MN Will (2E)	$16.95	

NEW YORK TITLES

Qty	ISBN	Title	Retail	Ext.
	1-57248-193-5	Child Custody, Visitation and Support in NY	$26.95	
	1-57248-141-2	How to File for Divorce in NY (2E)	$26.95	
	1-57248-105-6	How to Form a Corporation in NY	$24.95	
	1-57248-095-5	How to Make a NY Will (2E)	$16.95	
	1-57248-199-4	How to Start a Business in NY (2E)	$18.95	
	1-57248-198-6	How to Win in Small Claims Court in NY (2E)	$18.95	

Qty	ISBN	Title	Retail	Ext.
	1-57248-197-8	Landlords' Legal Guide in NY	$24.95	
	1-57071-188-7	New York Power of Attorney Handbook	$19.95	
	1-57248-122-6	Tenants' Rights in NY	$21.95	

NORTH CAROLINA TITLES

Qty	ISBN	Title	Retail	Ext.
	1-57248-185-4	How to File for Divorce in NC (3E)	$22.95	
	1-57248-129-3	How to Make a NC Will (3E)	$16.95	
	1-57248-184-6	How to Start a Business in NC (3E)	$18.95	
	1-57248-091-2	Landlords' Rights & Duties in NC	$21.95	

OHIO TITLES

Qty	ISBN	Title	Retail	Ext.
	1-57248-190-0	How to File for Divorce in OH (2E)	$24.95	
	1-57248-174-9	How to Form a Corporation in OH	$24.95	
	1-57248-173-0	How to Make an OH Will	$16.95	

PENNSYLVANIA TITLES

Qty	ISBN	Title	Retail	Ext.
	1-57248-242-7	Child Custody, Visitation and Support in Pennsylvania	$26.95	
	1-57248-211-7	How to File for Divorce in PA (3E)	$26.95	
	1-57248-094-7	How to Make a PA Will (2E)	$16.95	
	1-57248-112-9	How to Start a Business in PA (2E)	$18.95	
	1-57248-245-1	The Landlord's Legal Guide in PA	$24.95	

TEXAS TITLES

Qty	ISBN	Title	Retail	Ext.
	1-57248-171-4	Child Custody, Visitation, and Support in TX	$22.95	
	1-57248-172-2	How to File for Divorce in TX (3E)	$24.95	
	1-57248-114-5	How to Form a Corporation in TX (2E)	$24.95	
	1-57248-255-9	How to Make a TX Will (3E)	$16.95	
	1-57248-214-1	How to Probate and Settle an Estate in TX (3E)	$26.95	
	1-57248-228-1	How to Start a Business in TX (3E)	$18.95	
	1-57248-111-0	How to Win in Small Claims Court in TX (2E)	$16.95	
	1-57248-110-2	Landlords' Rights and Duties in TX (2E)	$21.95	

SUBTOTAL THIS PAGE _____

SUBTOTAL PREVIOUS PAGE _____

Shipping — $5.00 for 1st book, $1.00 each additional _____

Illinois residents add 6.75% sales tax _____

Connecticut residents add 6.00% sales tax _____

TOTAL _____

To order, call Sourcebooks at 1-800-432-7444 or FAX (630) 961-2168 (Bookstores, libraries, wholesalers—please call for discount)
Prices are subject to change without notice.
Find more legal information at: www.SphinxLegal.com